MY CCM SOUNDTRACKED LIFE

HOW I BECAME DISILLUSIONED WITH THE MUSIC THAT ONCE CAPTIVATED ME

JAMIE A. KOCUR

BROKEN FILTER MEDIA, LLC

For permission requests, write to the publisher at the address below:

Broken Filter Media, LLC
Attention: Permissions Coordinator
75 North Woodward Avenue #6728
Tallahassee, Florida 32313

www.brokenfiltermedia.com

ISBN: 978-1-952708-00-8 (softcover)
ISBN: 978-1-952708-01-5 (ebook)
v. 1.0.1

Love Can Turn the World
Benjamin Gaither, Jeff Silvey, Kim Williams

Love Can Turn the World
Benjamin Gaither, Jeff Sean Silvey, Kim Williams

Light Gives Heat
Charlie Lowell, Dan Haseltine, Matt Odmark, Stephen Daniel Mason

Blessed Be Your Name
Beth Redman, Matt Redman

Lead Me To The Cross
Brooke Ligertwood

Paradise Lost
Christopher John Cunningham and John Robert Harmanson

For Drew:

When you caught me crying
for the hundredth time after church
and listened yet again
to my frustrated venting, you told me,
"Sounds like you need to write a book."

CONTENTS

PRELUDE

Walking into the dimly-lit sanctuary, I coughed from the fog that descended upon the space. Colored lights were set dramatically at different angles on stage. Several guitars were propped up on stands, and the drum kit was boxed into a Plexiglas shell.

Someone commented behind me, “Is this worship or a Pink Floyd concert?” He and his friend laughed at the joke, but I uneasily asked myself the same question.

Worship began. Low, mellow music filled the air for a few measures while the stage lights slowly brought the band into view. Electric guitar riffs blared through the speaker directly over my head and catchy drumbeats brought everyone to their feet.

The worship leader rose to center stage and shouted, “WE WORSHIP YOU, JESUS!” His hands rose above his head, and he brought them together, encouraging everyone to join him. The congregation roared in approval. The sound of hands clapping, some slightly off beat, filled my ears.

I stood alone in the crowd, feeling like I was being swallowed. Tears pricked my eyes, but these were not the tears of gratefulness that I used to offer in worship. These were tears of frustration. I didn't feel worshipful. I felt empty.

"God," I whispered, "Where are You?"

I couldn't connect in worship anymore. I sang, clapped to the beat, closed my eyes to focus on the words—all the things I had done for years. I used to feel deeply connected with all the musical aspects of worship. The rhythm. The melodies. The lyrics. In recent months, things had begun to change.

The shift happened slowly. At first, I thought it was just an aversion to certain songs, and I would gently remind myself that worship is not about my preference. But with each passing Sunday, the aversion slowly grew into a full-fledged resentment.

The resentment felt like a huge wall. I envisioned one side of the wall to be a place where I had a beautifully-connected life with God, encouraged and fueled by musical worship. On the other side, there was only frustration, bitterness, and struggle. As soon as the music started, up went the wall. Most feeble attempts to connect were never successful. The words that used to touch my very soul now meant nothing and became a jumble on the PowerPoint screen. The melodies that had gracefully flowed from my vocal cords now grated on my nerves. The band that had once been filled with gracious and talented volunteers now only seemed like loud noise.

Standing on what I felt was the wrong side of the wall, I banged on the bricks, desperate to get to the other side. As I scraped my knuckles from the constant beating, I became cynical and critical. I stopped singing and judged every typo on the screen or missed note on stage. Each week, I walked away wondering what the point of it all was.

When did worship become a show? The music was filled with many of the same songs that had touched my heart for over ten years. This beautiful thing now felt like nothing more than weekly entertainment. I thought that I was being too judgmental. I searched my heart and tried to pray the cynicism away. But every time I said "Amen," I would open my eyes and still be face to face with the wall.

I used to thrive on musical worship. It was my lifeblood. I was one of those peppy singers at the front of the stage. If I wasn't on stage, I was in the front row with hands raised high to the heavens. Every worship song spoke directly to me. The words filled my heart. It was a love affair between my Savior and me, fueled by passionate love songs.

Now I can't shake the feeling that there is more to worship than this. Am I truly worshipping the Lord of creation through this music? Is this a genuine offering, or is it just something that fills me?

I kept coming back to the same question.

God, where *are* You in all this?

I used to be a worship leader, proudly singing praise songs from the front of the stage. Now I'm a doubter, cowering in the farthest back corner. I became aware of the performance aspect of worship and was unwilling to be a cast member in the vast production any longer. So I walked away from the stage and then began to question what the point of worship even was. As I struggled with the deconstruction of that pivotal piece of my life and faith, I felt helpless.

I prayed and processed and waited for the dramatic ah-ha moment that would magically fix everything and switch worship music from blah back to inspiring. I had an ah-ha moment, but it wasn't the one I was expecting.

After a couple years of desperate prayer and frustrated church attendance, I found that I was no closer to scaling the wall of resentment. I started writing to sort through the jumbled mess in my head. Writing has always been my medium to figure out what I'm thinking. I frantically journaled, pouring words onto the page in hopes that somewhere along the way, those words would fit together in a beautiful, cohesive way.

As I wrote and processed, little things clicked. I realized how sensitive I was to the production value of worship; how I'm an introvert and don't care for loud, upbeat worship; how I'd made worship music into my own personal idol.

These were all valuable pieces, but as I stepped back to look at the big picture I was surprised by what I saw. I found that I wasn't only resentful of worship music, I was angry with all of contemporary Christian culture.

After I had accepted Jesus at the age of 18, I became a goody two-shoes Christian. I read my Bible everyday, never drank or swore, and pledged to remain a virgin until marriage. I was super sensitive to all sin in my life, and I walked on eggshells around my carnal desires. I happily welcomed all things Christian into my life, especially music. I invited Contemporary Christian Music (CCM) to be my life's soundtrack.

The Christian subculture was safe: a warm, comfy bubble that enveloped Jesus and me. If people swore or told dirty jokes around me, I climbed on my mighty high horse and glared down upon them. If I heard something that didn't fit into the safe world I had made, I plugged my ears and ignored it. I had been saved and made clean. I couldn't fill my life with that filth. I surrounded myself with only holy, pure things. I took Philippians 4:8 to the extreme. I stayed in my safe bubble for ten years, happily oblivious to the real world around me.

Along the way I met the real world. I saw a bigger picture. In my Christian bubble, I had formed answers to neatly wrap up the hard questions in life. I slowly learned that's not how life works, that it's not always possible to wrap up the tough questions in a pretty package. I struggled with issues like homosexuality and the church's treatment of women. I watched as Christians responded to the world with hatred. Meanwhile I found atheists and agnostics who were living more Christ-like lives than those same Christians. I found non-Christian music that spoke more beautifully of my journey with Christ than the worship songs ever could. The ever-lasting peace that was promised through so many CCM songs became more and more elusive.

My comfy bubble popped. I landed on my butt, blinking in disbelief. The happy Christian world crumbled around me, leaving me in shell shock as I brushed off the pieces. I thought my Christian bubble was the way to live. I believed that by surrounding myself with music that only spoke of Jesus or by shopping in stores targeted to the Christian evangelical, I would be well. Saved. Blessed.

I now see Christian music as merely a marketing tool and Christian stores as irrelevant chains. I'm resentful. I'm shaking my fist at the church, screaming, "How dare you misguide me?"

I feel betrayed. I'm disillusioned with the church, with Christian subculture, with worship music, with every shiny piece of merchandise that states, "Jesus is the light of the world!"

It makes sense that my disillusionment would rear its ugly head with music. Music has been a driving force in my life. I believed that I would be using music to glorify Jesus for the rest of my life. It was to be my professional calling.

I'm stuck between two worlds now. One world is a blissful, contented relationship with God. The other acknowledges that I'm a little broken, filled with doubts and questions, wondering if this Christian life is worth it - and sometimes even if God is real. I long for the passion and conviction I felt for my faith, but I don't want to go back to being un-relatable and cut off from the world. I strive to be Christ-like, but I laugh at off-color jokes. I want to be on fire for Christ, but I don't want to be spewing Bible verses at people. I want to share the love of Jesus, but I don't want to come off as crazy or forceful. I want to sing, but I don't want to lead worship anymore.

This is my journey into the disillusionment, my discovery of it, and my attempt to process through it. This isn't a book of answers; it's mostly questions. Through those questions, I feel a little freer. I share them because reading other people's struggles has often brought me strength, the calm knowing that I'm not alone.

Announcing your brokenness does not mean giving up hope. I've found renewed hope in my brokenness.

May you find the same.

PART I

MELODY

1

STRANGE BLACK MARKINGS

Most of my early memories are a big blur of specific feelings and vague objects with no exact placement or context. Except for church. There, the memories are more vivid, more precise. They feel more real.

I was four, trying to sit through a long sermon that I couldn't understand. My older sister and I sat quietly. We scribbled on the blue prayer cards with the tiny golf pencils that were tucked in the back of the pew in front of us. I squirmed on the hard-backed pew, trying to find a comfortable spot. I peeked over the seat in front of me in an attempt to see the pastor, but the lady in front of me blocked my view. All I could see was frizzled white hair.

Letting out a quiet huff, I sank back down into the bench. I just wanted church to be over. It was so long and boring.

I believed in God. It seemed like something that should be believed in. When I looked at the world, I figured someone must be in charge of it. I never put much more thought into it than that.

My Sunday school teacher taught me about God. I learned some Bible stories, but the details were fuzzy. They all ran together. Something about a boat and animals and a rod and a cross, I think. Often those lessons simply confused me.

Sometimes lessons happened in big church. One Sunday, they called the children to gather at the front. I timidly walked toward the teacher, feeling vulnerable out from the safety of my mom's side. I peered up from under my long, brown bangs at the man in front of us. He smiled, a big, friendly beam that made me a little more comfortable.

He fiddled with a ring between his fingers. I watched it bounce and roll from finger to finger, shimmering from the light above us. Once we were silent, he began his lesson. He held up the ring and let us all get a good look.

"God has no beginning, and no end," he said. "No one created God. He has always been around. Like this ring, He is never ending. No beginning. No end."

He challenged us to find the beginning of the ring. Some children tried, with no success. I was baffled. How can something have no beginning? It had to start somewhere.

These lessons confused and intrigued me (I'm still trying to figure out that damn ring). I imagined that God must be pretty powerful. I envisioned Him as a big grandfather with a long, flowing beard, someone whose knee I could sit on and ask questions. Not that I would talk to Him. I was painfully shy and never spoke to anyone I didn't know. I couldn't even find my voice to tell Santa what I wanted for Christmas. God was too big and scary to speak to. I had stranger-danger even with God.

Each week, I sat through another sermon, trying to figure out what was going on. Big words flowed in and out of my head.

But after the long, boring, and confusing messages came the music. That was my favorite part. I loved when the pastor announced a page in the hymnal. I jumped up eagerly because I knew the service was drawing to a close. I stood on tiptoe next to my mother and peered intently at the Methodist hymnal in her hand. The organ played some long, loud tones, and I looked around. What was coming next?

Everyone began to sing. Together. All at once. I was amazed. How did they know when to start and what to sing? All I could see were strange black lines and markings on the page. It was like some code that everyone knew but me.

Each Sunday, I hoped that the unfamiliar markings would begin to make sense and I would be able to join. But no matter how hard I focused on the hymnal, it never became any clearer. I gave up and simply listened to the voices around me. I looked up at the faces as they sang. The women smiled, at peace with the world.

I couldn't understand most of the words they sang, more big words that my little brain couldn't wrap around. But there was something special about the sound. I longed to sing with them.

I did sing, eventually. Even though I was shy and a little scared, my parents made me join the children's choir. We worked for weeks preparing "Away in a Manger" for the congregation.

I wore a scratchy white robe and a red bowtie. The choir director tried to straighten all our robes and tighten the ties, all while keeping us in line and quiet. Although we were only vaguely aware of what we were about to do, we sensed that it was important.

We paraded out of the back room and onto the stage. People clapped and aww-ed at us as the director shuffled the stragglers back into place. She took her place in front of the choir and with a big grin reminded us to keep our eyes on her. The piano played the intro, and we launched into the song that we had rehearsed over and over.

We sang "Away in a Manger" in our sweet, little, off-key voices. We sang loud, missed a few cues, smiled our toothy grins, and the boy next to me waved at mom. The people applauded loudly when we finished.

I have a fondness for that sweet lullaby to this day. That melody has been embedded in my brain for as long as I can remember. When I hear that song now, I'm transported to the front of a congregation, next to a big, lit-up Christmas tree covered in white, crocheted angels.

I wasn't aware, but the seeds of worship and music were being planted in my growing heart.

2

WHISPERY PAGES

"If you ever feel like you have no other place to go, you can always go to church," my mom told me. I nodded like I understood, but this lesson wouldn't make sense until years later.

Ironically, a year after my mom told me this, we stopped attending church. Due to a couple of cross-country moves, we fell out of church attendance for a while. My dad's job as a bridge engineer required him to be where the work was, so we packed up the house and trekked across the states, screaming cats and clueless dog stuffed into our minivan. After the first move from Georgia to Arizona, my father was told we wouldn't be there long. Sure enough, a year and a half later, we moved again.

Since we were still unpacking and then repacking, we never settled back into church. It wasn't a conscious decision on my parents' part. I'm sure they were exhausted from all the craziness. I didn't mind. No hard pews or long sermons to sit through and an extra morning to play. I didn't even miss church.

But once we were settled in Florida, we had no excuses

anymore... except that habits are hard to break, and the practice of not going to church continued. We were in Florida for years before we made an effort to attend again.

It was Mom that dragged us back. Mom's best high school friend was diagnosed with cancer. Mom sent letters of support and called her often. And with the sweet, childlike faith that my mother has always possessed, she prayed. Actually, she gave God an ultimatum. She told God that if He would heal her friend, we would go back to church.

God held up His end of the bargain. And Mom sure wasn't backing out on hers.

We found a Methodist church close to home. Sighing, I walked in with memories of long, boring sermons and big spiritual words. The pews were just as hard as I remembered.

I was mostly unimpressed with the whole experience, at least initially. I liked communion Sunday because the sermon was a few minutes shorter. I didn't understand the significance of the ceremony, but I enjoyed the cute cups of grape juice.

Then, there was the music. It still drew me in.

The organ began with a few long chords, and then the piano joined in, doubling the chords and playing the melody. The tinkling of the keys made me anticipate the beginning of the verse. The bearded man at the front smiled at the congregation before him as he lifted his arms, signaling our entrance. Over the top of blue hymnals, voices lifted in unison and then slipped into harmonies. The music surrounded my ears and made my head buzz happily. The choir sang out from the choir loft, and for a moment, I found myself wishing I could adorn one of the flowy robes, singing out to the people gathered before God.

Music hadn't taken its hold on my life yet, but it was starting to pique my interest. Though I still didn't understand the musical part of the hymnal, I could now read the words, and I began to catch onto familiar melodies.

There was still something mystical about those blue, hard-bound books. I liked the thin, whispery pages and the stanzas of music. I liked to look at the music notes scattered over the pages. I read the words, confused as to their meaning. They still sounded pretty.

When the organ began playing and the entire congregation began in unison, I listened in awe. I was able to join in now, but I still felt like that four year old staring up at everyone, spellbound.

The melodies that circled through the air around my head followed me out of church. They weren't going to let me be.

3

SOLO & ENSEMBLE

One day during my traumatizing middle school years, I walked out of the bathroom. A girl was standing there as if waiting on me.

"Hi Jamie!" she said in a particularly sing-songy voice.

"Hi," I responded hesitantly. I was suspicious. She had never been outright mean but was never warm-hearted toward me either. I was drowning in insecurity, and I was suspicious of any popular person acknowledging me. My back faced the bathroom door as it swung closed. She smiled big and put a hand on my shoulder, inching me away from the door.

"Here, come with me," she crooned, still giving me a smile I wasn't sure I could trust. I let her pull me away from the door. Suddenly, she stuck a maxi pad to my back then ran away giggling. Tears stung my eyes as I tried to reach over my shoulder to pull it off, hoping no one had seen. Luckily, it wasn't used.

I was deeply insecure and floated through most of my preteen years trying not to be noticed. I preferred a low profile to being teased. I watched all of the cool kids around me, longing to fit in. Like every other adolescent, I just longed for acceptance, even from the cruel kids around me. I didn't possess the confidence so many others around me seemed to have. I wished that I could dress like them, laugh like them, rake my hand through my long hair and let it fall decadently over my shoulders. I tried to buy cool clothes or do my hair like they did, but it never worked. My clothes always felt dorky, my laugh awkward, and my hair thick and tangled.

I finally found confidence in a way I wasn't expecting.

All the students in my school filled one free period with an elective class: band, chorus, shop, or graphic arts. I tried band for a few weeks and was crushed when I wasn't allowed to play flute because all the cool girls had already picked the flute. Instead, I was given the oboe. I hated that dumb instrument. I never could get the air to flow through the reed the right way and was always penalized by an annoying buzzing on my lips. After that disappointing experience, I tried chorus.

I ended up in chorus not for a love of music but because it seemed the best (or easiest - I didn't think there would be much mental energy expended toward it) choice for my middle school elective class. Also, my friends were there. Strength in numbers usually wins out.

I sat in choir surrounded by my peers, singing in unison and occasional off-key harmony. It was a fun way to pass the last hour in my school day and a nice break from note taking and tests. We sang weird warm ups and songs I had never heard.

Every spring, my fellow choristers grew excited about Solo and Ensemble, a festival where singers and instrumentalists came to share the music they had worked on for months. The bravest of the brave stepped out in front of judges and performed a song they had learned and memorized. Not me. No way would I sing by myself, especially not in front of a judge. I was content to stay hidden among all the other voices, singing soft enough to not stick out. Secretly, I longed to sing at Solo and Ensemble, but fear kept me silent.

In my eighth grade year, my friends wanted to do a song for Solo and Ensemble, and they asked me to be a part of it. Six girls total: two on first soprano, two on second soprano, and two on alto. I had watched other brave singers longingly from a distance for too long. I decided to do it. Besides, I wasn't singing by myself. I was safely surrounded by five friends, nestled securely among other voices.

Mrs. Prescott, our chorus teacher, picked a piece for us entitled "Johnny Has Gone For a Soldier." I was assigned the alto part. I think that was the first and last time I ever sang alto.

Disheartened, I looked over my boring part. One line was the same note repeated over and over. The first sopranos excitedly bragged about their part. I pouted. The melody was the important part.

I learned that alto part, and it grew on me. What had once been a repetitive line of the same note was now a chance to work on dynamics. I had never sung an alto part before, and I loved the rich tone that came out of me. I began to see how all parts are important and the way each one contributes to the song. Combined, they are a beautiful, cohesive mix.

With just a few rehearsals left until the big performance, Mrs. Prescott pulled us into the cramped practice room to run through the song. With seven of us in the confined space, we were practically sitting on the upright piano. I stood directly behind my teacher, not realizing how close I was to her ears. I sang with gusto.

As Mrs. Prescott hit the last chord, she turned around and looked me straight in the eye. "Jamie! I had no idea you could sing like that! It was beautiful!"

I could feel my face flush as I thanked her for the compliment.

Really? I can sing?

PART II

HARMONY

4

MOUNTAINSIDE DANCE

"So, um... do you want to go to the banquet with me?" Danny had just finished telling me about the Mu Alpha Theta, or math club, banquet. I was being asked out on a date but was too terrified to admit it. I could feel my heart begin to race, and my palms became clammy. I tried to think of a way to politely decline. My insecurities had followed me into high school, and that timidity flowed into my love life, or lack thereof. In my mind, there was no way a guy could be interested in me.

In the end, I couldn't think of a good excuse, so I agreed to go, making it obvious that it was as friends.

My freshman year of high school didn't do any favors for my deep insecurities. Many of my middle school friends went to other high schools, and those that went to the same school had differing schedules. I found myself alone a lot and spent most of my freshman year wallowing in self-pity.

I made new friends but still watched the cool girls from a distance. Better dressed than me, they possessed the elusive self-confidence I had never been able to obtain. They weren't blatantly mean to me like middle-school, maxi-pad girl, but the way they ignored my presence felt almost as bad. I still desperately longed for acceptance.

I ironically found it at the Mu Alpha Theta banquet.

Danny's dad drove us to the banquet while we sat awkwardly in the back seat. I kept my hands folded in my lap, my head facing the front of the car. We made uncomfortable small talk, and I wished I had come up with an excuse to get out of the evening. Danny was an incredibly sweet guy, but I had no idea what to do in a date-like situation. Even though I had stressed the friends part when accepting the invite, I wasn't sure what Danny was thinking. My shyness was in full force.

Once we got to the banquet and settled into our seats, slurping spaghetti and red sauce into our mouths, I relaxed. I chatted with Brianne, who sat at the same table with us. She was sweet and very welcoming. We laughed about how hard it was to eat spaghetti neatly. I looked around the room and saw a couple people I recognized. Everyone seemed at ease with each other.

I watched these socially-awkward people who somehow possessed a certain confidence. I fit in immediately. I didn't feel like I had to prove myself around them. And as thankful as I was for the invite that Danny had extended to join this group of misfit people, our relationship never moved past friendship. He proved to be one of my most loyal friends through my next three years of high school.

The next year I joined Mu Alpha Theta. I had never been particularly good at math, but that didn't seem to matter. I felt like I was finally part of a cool club, even if those outside the club made fun of us.

Math nerds are typical high school students, so it was teenage drama at it's finest. There was always gossip about who was dating whom, and it seemed like one new relationship sprang up at every competition. I met my first two boyfriends through Mu Alpha Theta.

I threw all I had into that club, attending every competition I could. I studied hard, desperate to win a trophy. The best competitions were nationals. We took weeklong trips to some really fun places. My favorite was a summer trip to Maine.

We stayed in a skiing lodge at the base of big, beautiful Sugarloaf Mountain. After a week of hard testing and awards ceremonies, we finished with a traditional Mu Alpha Theta dance.

The dance was outside with the shadow of the mountain looming over us in the darkness. The DJ played all the popular favorites like "Gangsta's Paradise" by Coolio and "Hold Me, Thrill Me, Kiss Me, Kill Me" by U2. The mob of teenagers pulsed and moved to the beat. Despite my quiet nature, I loved a good dance. When I was surrounded by the safety of friends, I could really get into it.

I started the evening on the outskirts, barely moving along to the beat in a circle of a few friends who were obviously ready for bed. I watched them yawn and looked longingly toward the center of pulsing teenagers. The fun was obviously being had in the middle, not on the fringes. Plus, I had seen a guy that I was crushing on move toward the middle. I wanted to follow but didn't want to be obvious.

Our friend Darren danced his way over to us. I laughed silently at his dance move attempts. "HEY!" he shouted at us. One of my girlfriends rolled her eyes.

"Hey!" I shouted back, trying to be heard over the deafening beats.

He moved toward my side, and another ridiculous move popped from his hips. This time, I laughed out loud.

Suddenly, he grabbed my hand and pulled me into the crowd. "C'mon!" he yelled before I could protest. We slid through throngs of sweaty teenagers gyrating together to the beat. I looked back at my friends to see if anyone was following us, but they weren't even looking our way.

We stopped at a crowd of fellow classmates. Some I knew well; others were upperclassmen that I didn't associate with much. And there was my crush. I glanced at Darren who shot me a knowing look. Apparently, my subtlety hadn't been so subtle that week.

I felt a little out of place, and for a moment, wistfully longed for the safety of the outskirts. My classmates didn't seen to notice my hesitancy. They shouted louder and danced harder.

"WOOOOOO!!!!" I watched in amazement as the class brainiac moved in ways I had never seen him move. His large, bottle-cap glasses fogged slightly from the heat of the crowd. His brown-colored forehead and neck had beads of sweat. He bent lower to the ground, his hips swinging and arms waving above his head. His t-shirt formed pools of sweat around the armpits.

Before too long, I let my inhibitions fly. I let loose and enjoyed the night. Every bit of insecurity flew away. I felt confident that I impressed the upperclassmen with my sense of rhythm. I even flirted with my crush. Darren smiled smugly to himself.

Another song began to play, "Closer" by Nine Inch Nails. The DJ started by muting the profane chorus but soon realized that the teenagers were shouting it at the top of their lungs. He gave up and turned up the volume.

Echoing off the mountainside, the words rattled my whole body.

This song had always made me nervous whenever I heard it on the radio. I liked the music, but the lyrics made me blush, especially the word "fuck." I was incredibly innocent. Although I understood the mechanics behind the phrase of the chorus, I definitely couldn't relate to the passion of it. I had stayed in denial about what the song was really about. Whenever the song came on while in mixed company, I had pretended to be interested in something else. It always felt like that awkward moment when a sex scene comes on in the movie you're watching with your parents.

Yet now, in the shadow of the mountain, I sang and shouted along with all the other teenagers. My conscience wouldn't let me sing that one word, but I found that I wasn't blushing. I was too focused on the energy surrounding me. I raised my arms and moved along with the throng of bodies. The intensity was amazing. The song seemed to grow louder and louder. People jumped up and down and screamed with increasing force.

The song ended, but the energy remained. We continued to dance into the night. I let go of all inhibitions and danced and screamed along with the rest of the crowd.

After the dance, I felt a renewed confidence. The upperclassmen now recognized me and even waved hello in the hall when we returned to school. Less than three months later, my crush and I were dating. It was as if the simple act of dancing had released my inhibitions and insecurities. The music that surrounded me that night had freed me somehow.

And yet, the coarseness and overly sexual lyrics of Nine Inch Nails continued to bother me. I felt a twinge of guilt when I thought back to how freely I had danced and sang along to "Closer." I tried to shake it, but the guilt continued to follow me, niggling away at the back of my brain.

5

MUSICAL SAFETY NET

"Loser" by Beck played through the stereo. My friends bobbed their heads along to the music, seemingly oblivious to the lyrics that played. In the chorus, Beck was basically asking for death.

Really?, I thought. *That seems... excessive.* Much like Nine Inch Nails, I liked Beck's music but struggled with the lyrics.

Throughout high school, I kept up with popular music. At parties, I would bob my head along to the beat and mouth the words. I felt cool. I pretended like I was totally fine with the curse words and negative messages. I didn't want to be the freak in the room.

I was conflicted. When I really listened to the songs of my high school years, they confused me. I couldn't understand the lyrics, and those I did understand were not the most uplifting. One day, while riding to school with a friend, "Bullet with Butterfly Wings" by Smashing Pumpkins came on the radio.

The image of the world as a vampire bothered me. I thought of all the happiness being drained from my life by the world around me, and I frowned. I didn't like that visual. And what was up with all his pent up rage? I wouldn't have minded if the radio channel was changed, but I was embarrassed to admit it to my friends. I bummed rides to school and listened to whatever was played.

I soon found an easy way out of music I couldn't fully comprehend.

My friend Claire invited me to her church's youth group. I was too shy to join the youth group at my own church, but I willingly accepted Claire's invitation. I found it easier to try something new with a trusted friend by my side.

The teenagers there accepted me much like my math club friends. Many of the youth group attendees were quirky and a little weird, but they all seemed confident in their oddity. I found it refreshing.

We played games and sat through short Bible lessons. The lessons were easier to understand than the sermons in church, but the gospel story was still hazy. They would pray, "Lord Jesus, thank You for dying for us." I didn't understand the cross, and I would scratch my head curiously as they prayed these things.

Everyone at youth group listened to contemporary Christian music, which I soon learned was referred to as CCM. I had never heard these songs, and I listened with interest as they played each week. These kids were listening to lots of this Jesus music. There were tons of Christian bands that I had never heard of: dcTalk, Audio Adrenaline, Newsboys.

As we mingled at the end of a meeting, one of these albums would play in the background. Every teenager in the room bopped their head along to the beat and silently mouthed the words. I felt a little left out. Then Claire loaned me her dcTalk *Free at Last* cassette tape.

"Thanks!" I was growing more curious about this new genre of music.

That night I slipped the cassette into my tape player. A

strong, steady beat began. Rap intertwined with melodies and harmonies. My foot began tapping along.

As soon as side one finished, I flipped the tape over and played side two. Then replayed side one. And replayed side two. Repeat. Over and over. I sang along to every song, even the raps.

The music was catchy, and the words were positive. I didn't feel guilty listening to it like I often did with other music. There were no dirty words, sexual phrases to make me blush, or negative messages. Secular music made me feel icky. I was a very conservative teenager, not interested in partying, doing drugs, or sleeping around. Much of the secular music I listened to was focused on this lifestyle, and I felt that by listening to it I was showing the world that I approved of it.

I remembered that muggy August night in the shadow of the Maine mountainside. Maybe I should have stayed on the sidelines rather than dancing along with a song that espoused a lifestyle I couldn't endorse. I thought of the sexual actions that "Closer" spoke of, and I shuddered. It wasn't something I should be focusing on as a sixteen year old. I wasn't ashamed of dancing, of letting go my inhibitions in that moment. I just wished it could have been to different music.

I sang along with the secular songs because they were catchy. I listened to secular music because it was popular. Those didn't seem like very good reasons anymore. I looked beyond the cool sound the songs emanated and toward the words they were speaking. If not geared toward sex, the lyrics usually focused on anger and angst. The lead singers had lots of emotions, and few were positive. They seemed like they had been hurt deeply by someone or something. As unresolved resentments tend to do, these hurts had festered, and now the musicians were bursting, screaming their discontent with the world.

In other songs, there were the curse words, which were

used in excess and contributed nothing to the song. I had always been sensitive to swear words, and every time I heard the word "fuck" I cringed. It was such a harsh word, and I grew tired of songs that relied on it for shock factor. Even if the words were bleeped on the radio, the jarring beep made me grate my teeth in annoyance.

Soon that dcTalk tape was the only album in my cassette deck. After finding another album by dcTalk, I played that one over and over. I couldn't get enough.

For my birthday, my friend Travis excitedly handed me a package. "Open it! Open it!" He jumped up and down.

I opened it to discover a CD. Travis grinned, "I know you've been really into dcTalk, so I thought you might like this guy."

I pulled the plastic wrap off and gazed at the soft brown cover. There was a man staring intently at the camera with his guitar propped against him. He had a kind smile on his face. I felt like he was saying, "I know something you don't."

I looked at the title. *The Great Adventure.*

"Thanks!" I grinned at Travis.

I popped *The Great Adventure* into my player, and it didn't come out of the machine for another month. I played it constantly on repeat. Steven Curtis Chapman quickly became my favorite artist. It didn't hurt that Toby Mac from dcTalk had a cameo in one of the songs.

I enjoyed the music, but the lyrics in particular compelled me. He really did know something I didn't. I had gone to church for years. I believed in God, but he spoke of a faith that was lived everyday. He sang of a Savior that changed him completely. There was a peace and a passion evident throughout the album, and I longed for it. The last song on the album, "Heart's Cry," especially tugged at my soul. It was a tender testimony set to music, and it brought tears to my eyes. I wanted to know this Jesus more fully too.

Suddenly all the secular songs on the radio scared me. They

felt dangerous. I thought of Beck singing for someone to kill him. He was clearly dealing with some insecurity and was entertaining the thought of death. I thought of my own insecurities and what could happen if I didn't deal with them. Would I end up like him? If I remained in this place, feeling so unsure of myself, would I too be longing for suicide? If I continued to fuel this fear of never fitting in with this angsty music, where might it lead me?

I thought of Kurt Cobain, the lead singer of Nirvana, who had committed suicide just two years prior. I hadn't listened very closely to many Nirvana songs, but the few lyrics I caught told me that Kurt had not been singing of the joys in his life. The themes in this music seemed to be depression and anger. I no longer wanted to surround my life with those subjects. I sometimes felt snippets of loneliness and depression through my desperate attempts to fit in at school. I never once considered suicide, but I feared what might happen if I continued to immerse myself in this kind of music.

I looked through my CD collection and was ashamed at what was there. I took all my secular CDs and sold them. I felt cleaner after I purged my collection. I had never understood Alanis Morisette and her *Jagged Little Pill* anyway.

I decided to settle into the safety of contemporary Christian music. In this safe haven, I didn't feel that God was shaking His head at my music choices, greatly disappointed in me. I also felt self-assurance in who I was. People may not accept me in high school, but Jesus Christ loved me as I was.

I was coming to faith gradually. As I listened to Christian music, the meaning behind all the cryptic sermons through the years began to make sense. I understood the cross and why it was so important. Jesus came to earth and died for my sins, and by believing in Him, I am saved.

The more Christian music I listened to, the more I began to understand about faith. And the more I understood, the more I wanted to understand. I knew that I needed to read the Bible. I had one but hadn't done much more than page through it in the six years I had it.

I had been ten when I had received that Bible. My mom had given it to me for Christmas, a King James Bible with a beautiful white cover and golden edged pages. I had always treasured that book. It was my very own Bible, and it sat on my nightstand, the prized spot that it deserved. Even before I understood it, I had sensed that book was holy and important, and I was honored to have one all my own.

I picked that golden edged book off my nightstand and began to read. I made the mistake of trying to read it like a regular book, starting at the beginning. The old English of the King James confused me, but I pushed through. I made it through Genesis and then Exodus. I gave up on Leviticus about ten chapters in.

I grew discouraged. I wanted to read the Bible, but I couldn't understand it. I tried other parts of the King James Version. The Psalms at least sounded pretty in the old English. The birth story of Jesus in Matthew and Luke was familiar and comforting. But still, none of it made sense.

One day, I stumbled across a New International Version translation of the Bible. It was packed in a box, something my sister had picked up during her college days. I think someone on campus had handed it to her on her way to class one day. It beckoned to me. I picked up the thick paperback and paged through it. I read a couple of passages. Closing the soft pages, I retreated to my room.

This time, instead of trying to read it from cover to cover, I started in the New Testament. I read the stories of Jesus.

Man, this guy is intriguing. I felt like I was reading a really good novel.

Every time I thought I knew how Jesus was going to react, He surprised me. He was unpredictable. I cheered at some stories, like when the woman caught in adultery was brought to Jesus and He refused to cast the first stone (John 8:1-11).

I frowned in utter confusion as I read other stories, like the possessed man who Jesus healed by sending his demons into a herd of pigs, which then careened off a cliff (Mark 5:1-20). I considered myself an animal rights activist. As I read the story I was struck not by the mercy offered to the man but only by the injustice done to the pigs.

I took that Bible to college, reading between classes. I curled up in the student lounge and pulled it into my lap, poring over passages in the gospels and highlighting my favorite parts. It was a fascinating read. I didn't want to put it down.

I was working my way toward the Christian definition of "saved." I never had that dramatic conversion experience, where everything becomes crystal clear and I invite Jesus into my heart with tears streaming down my face. It was more a slow realization that I needed Jesus. It was a process.

Music helped with that process. Music is the tool that God used to reach me. It helped establish the ground for my faith. I used to say, "Music saved me." I thought it sounded dramatic when in reality it was a really dangerous statement.

In time, I took that music and turned it into an idol. I used Christian music to build up a safe wall around me, one that kept the world at bay.

6

WARM FUZZIES

"It's a week-long festival with bands and awesome artists and Christian speakers and music and more music, and oh my goodness we HAVE to go!!!"

Travis bounced up and down as he spewed off his long run-on sentence. It was our freshman year in college at Florida State University, and we shared a couple classes together. After he had given me that Steven Curtis Chapman CD in high school, we had bonded through Christian music.

"So can we go? CAN WE GO????"

He was talking about Creation, a Christian music festival in Pennsylvania. It was four days of non-stop Christian bands and speakers.

"Travis, it sounds awesome, but how are we going to get there?"

We had kept in touch with Derek, another high school friend who was at Georgia Tech. Travis and Derek were my closest Christian friends. Our friendship bonded even more that year, despite Derek being hours away. We would send countless emails to each other, telling college stories and venting about hard classes. We shared the latest band that we were into and how our favorite Christian songs had touched our heart. Travis and I spent many an hour at the computer lab together, one screen away from each other, laughing out loud at the emails we sent to our trio. Two hundred sixty miles away, Derek would be at another computer and would quickly reply to our email, sending back a response within minutes. I spent more time emailing friends than studying at that computer lab.

When we told Derek about Creation, he thought it was a great idea. Now, we just had to figure out how to get there.

We were three broke 19-year-olds. How in the heck would we make a 2,000-mile round trip from Florida into the mountains of Pennsylvania? None of us had a car reliable enough to make the trip. I had just bought my first car, an '89 Ford Tempo with no air conditioning. As proud as I was of that car there was no way it could make it.

Derek returned home for the summer. Our trio was inseparable those three months, and the thought of taking a road trip together made us giddy. We brainstormed, trying to figure out how we would get from Tallahassee, Florida to Mt. Union, Pennsylvania. We were determined. It was four days of nonstop concerts, inspirational talks, and camping. How could we possibly miss it?

"We could rent a car!" Travis exclaimed.

Derek shot him a look. "You have to be 25. We're nowhere near the age limit."

Travis deflated a little but still looked determined. He did some research and found a local car place that would rent to 18 year olds. Lucky's Car Rental. It was a pretty sketchy place, but we didn't care. It was our ticket to Creation.

We rented some kind of four-door sedan. It wasn't the nicest car. It also wasn't the most reliable. On the way home that darn thing practically overheated, causing us to pull over and panic at a McDonald's. We prayed for God to help the car since we were all clueless on what to do. So God sent hail. It did cool the car down.

As scary as that car was, it got us to Pennsylvania. It was our own little Godsend. We loaded that thing down with luggage and camping equipment. We didn't have enough room in the trunk, so we strapped a carrier to the roof. It looked like a turtle when we were done. I'm surprised it didn't topple over from the weight.

By this time, we had picked up another traveler. Bob was an acquaintance from our high school social circle. While chatting with Derek one day, he found out that we were going to Creation. He had wanted to go to the festival for years and begged to come with us. Actually, I think he ended up inviting himself, and Derek didn't know how to say no. I was a little disappointed that our threesome turned to four. I had been looking forward to quality time with my two best friends. It also meant a bit more luggage to cram into our tiny sedan, but at least it gave us another driver and a little extra help footing the car rental bill.

We were so excited about our road trip adventure. I laughed at the fact that I was the only girl and braced myself for a week of boy noises. We printed out a banner that read, "Creation or BUST!" and taped it to the car top carrier. We stuffed ourselves into the tiny sedan, armfuls of CDs in hand for the trip, and away we went.

It was a long, two-day car ride. We busied ourselves by playing the alphabet game and name that tune. Travis and Derek challenged me to see if I could still do the rap from "Jesus is Just Alright" by dcTalk. I could. From memory.

As we got farther north, I began to revel in the mountains and foothills. The roads became more curvy and winding. The foothills and mountains took my mind off my boredom and into myself, contemplating the vastness of the universe and the nature of God that was becoming more familiar. Beauty all around made me forget the four walls of the suffocating car.

After two long days, we arrived at the gates. We were so excited we could barely stand it. Unfortunately, it was raining. Pouring, actually. The campground, now a running river of mud, couldn't let anyone in until the rain slowed down.

Trapped in a line of parked cars, I focused on the rain pelting the car. It soothed my anxiousness and took my mind off the fact that we were not getting any closer to point B. Derek laid his head against the window, mouth wide open and tongue sticking out, catching water droplets on his tongue. Water was dripping into our ghetto rental car. Fantastic.

In the front seat, Bob played with Dotty, my Dalmatian Beanie Baby. He spoke in a high-pitched voice and moved her paws back and forth. I smiled at his ventriloquist attempt.

Travis, the most eager of us to get out of the car, gripped the steering wheel and bounced in the driver's seat. Unable to sit still, he turned the windshield wipers on. And off. On. Off.

"Our sign is probably ruined," he stated in between wiper blade swipes.

I sighed and made a pouty face. "There goes our photo op."

We had received several honks from passing cars during our two-day road trip because of that sign. Now it was probably streaked beyond recognition. I had hoped to get a picture of all of us standing by it once we got to our campsite.

Sighing, I leaned against the backseat window and gazed out at the rain. It fell harder, and the line of vehicles remained immobile.

Finally, mercifully, the rain slowed down. We drove through muddy green fields filled with tents and pop up campers. Arriving at our camp spot, we gratefully sprang from our two-day confinement. I discovered that although worse for wear, our sign was still legible enough for the photo I had hoped for.

A kind neighbor offered to take the picture, and then we set to the task of setting up camp.

Camp was cozy. Three cute little tents and lawn chairs surrounded the Coleman stove I borrowed from my father. We had a homey little area, and I was excited about the prospect of living here for a week. The excitement in my stomach grew some more. Away from home, with an entire week of concerts in front of me... I couldn't have been happier.

With camp complete, Derek and I went in search of a phone to call home and let concerned parents know we had arrived safely. It was 1998, and none of us had cell phones.

We trekked all over Creation (pun intended), and before we found the pay phones, we wandered into the music store. Suddenly, miles of sparkling jewel cases surrounded us. Derek got a frenzied look in his eyes. All that new music was calling his name.

"I gotta get outta here!" He sprinted from the store with incredible speed. He dashed away like a deer desperately trying to escape its hunter.

I laughed as I tried to keep up with him. The temptation was just too much. Christian music had become a big obsession for us, and our part-time jobs could barely keep up with our college expenses, let alone the CDs that continually called our names. Being at a Christian music festival was only going to fuel that passion.

After a long, hot afternoon of waiting, it was finally time for the concerts. We had our spot picked out on the big hill in front of the stage. Our blanket spread on the grass was barely big enough to fit the four of us. The guys started wrestling in their impatience, and I got shoved into the dirt. I picked myself up, dusted off my leg, and rolled my eyes.

Lights dimmed, and the concerts began. We jumped to our feet and began to cheer and scream in response to the guitar chords and drumbeats that echoed through the valley. One after the other, bands took the stage. Big Tent Revival, Delirious, Rebecca St. James. The music made me feel alive, and I laughed and sang along with my friends.

The final show of the evening, The Supertones, took the stage. I loved the energy of the show with horns and catchy rhythms. We all got up and danced on our blanket, partly to keep warm from the sudden temperature drop.

The music stopped, and there was quiet as the lead singer walked onto stage with acoustic guitar in hand. He began to softly sing "Shout to the Lord" and invited us to join him.

With my eyes closed tight, my hands tentatively rose to the sky.

Shout to the Lord, all the earth let us sing...

He asked us to kneel with him. I dropped to the dirt and felt the wetness of the accumulating dew wash over my kneecaps. With eyes still closed, he led us in prayer. I felt something stirring inside me, and butterflies filled my stomach. Tears began to prick my eyes. I gave into them, and soon full teardrops were falling down my cheek.

Power and majesty, praise to the King...

Crying harder, my hands lifted higher. This God that had been gradually inching closer to me felt closer than ever. I uttered out a silent prayer of thanksgiving and awe as my teardrops hit the mud below.

Mountains bow down and the trees will roar
at the sound of Your name...

I thanked God over and over. I was ready to serve Him with

my whole heart. As I sang the words to the chorus over and over, I could feel my heart melting and accepting God fully.

That was my first mountaintop experience, when God became more real than I'd ever felt Him. I was ready to turn every aspect of my life over to Him: my thoughts, my outward actions, and my words. I was ready to show the world that I served a gracious, loving, and powerful God. That was the moment where I really let God in and fully committed my life to Him. Up until that point, I'd been a little hesitant. Creation showed me it was time to take the plunge.

Mountaintop moments are a beautiful experience, one that most Christians have at least once. It may or may not involve music, but it definitely makes it more dramatic with a soundtrack.

I am thankful for that summer at Creation. That festival helped cement my faith. But I let myself believe some things that would not always hold true. And some things are hard to unlearn.

PART III

CRESCENDO

7

WANNABE CHRISTIAN DIVA

The spotlights brightened as the house dimmed. Deafening applause filled my ears as Steven Curtis Chapman took the stage. He waved to the crowd as he stepped to the microphone. His southern drawl filled the room.

"How you doin', Pensacola?"

The crowd roared in response as the band began their first song. It was three months after Creation. Travis, Derek, and I jumped at the chance for another Christian concert, this time only hours away. We sprang to our feet and clapped along. I grew more and more entranced with each song, my eyes glued to the stage. I took in the bright lights, the guitars, the microphones, and Steven on center stage.

I sang every word to every song. "Let Us Pray" energized me and had me jumping up and down while "Free" made me want to fall to my knees. I was drawn in by the way that Steven was lifting up God through music, invigorating and convicting the crowd before him. I watched as the people around me closed their eyes and raised their hands. They were captivated by the music and were worshipping God through it.

Toward the end of the concert, he began "Amazing Grace," inviting everyone to sing along. I huddled together with Travis and Derek, and we sang. Hands draped over each other's shoulders, we swayed to the rhythm. I closed my eyes.

I forgot everyone around me, and I sang loudly, praising God. My mind drifted to my life and how I was serving God, or rather how I wasn't serving God enough. I had been attending church and Wednesday night Bible study but hadn't progressed much beyond that. I wasn't volunteering or serving at church or anywhere else, and I felt convicted by that. I wanted to help people, and I was beginning to think that I could do that through music.

Music had become my love. Melodies coursed through my veins, and I longed to let them out. My voice felt as if it had been stifled and kept silent for too long. I wanted to sing.

I want to sing for God. I want to write melodies and songs that honor Him.

I looked back toward the stage.

I want to do that. I'm going to be a Christian singer-songwriter.

As I stood in that pew, pulsing music surrounding me, I made an action plan to move toward my goal. I chose the next logical step, changing my major to music.

If I had any idea in that moment how hard the next few years would be, I wouldn't have made that choice. In the passion of the moment, all I could think about was being on stage and singing for God.

On the long ride back home, Travis turned around and looked at me in the back seat.

"Y'know, I was thinking earlier how you always sing so soft. If you sang like me, it'd be like, 'Wow!'"

Derek and I caught each other's eyes in the rearview mirror and chuckled. The only singing volumes Travis had were loud and louder. He sang loudly and often drifted off pitch on purpose for comedic effect.

He smiled and continued, "No, seriously, while we sang "Amazing Grace" tonight, I could hear you. And I was thinking, 'Wow! Jamie can sing!'"

I blushed and thanked Travis. He gave me one of his huge, encouraging grins. I grinned back. He turned toward the front, jumping in his seat, still energized from the show.

I took Travis's encouraging comment as a sign that my revelation was truly from God.

EAGER FOR WAYS TO practice music and to serve, I joined the chancel choir at church. Three months after the Steven Curtis Chapman concert, on a cold January evening, I timidly walked through the choir room doors. My former high school choir directors, Doc and his wife Miss Bobbie, welcomed me. Miss Bobbie enveloped me in one of her big hugs that I had grown to love so much. Doc grinned wide when he saw me. There was pride in his voice as he introduced me as one of his former students.

I collected music and joined the soprano section. I made polite conversation with a fellow choir member until rehearsal began. The choir was beginning work on its Easter cantata, and I paged through the thick music with interest. There were several solos, and I entertained the thought of auditioning. We received a cassette of the cantata for extra practice. I listened to it in my car on my way to and from classes. I learned the soprano part quickly and then fell in love with a soprano/tenor duet.

The song featured Mary Magdalene and Jesus at the empty tomb, the resurrection story I had especially grown to love from John 20. The song started out somber and mellow and then crescendoed into a glorious, happy conclusion. The soprano part was one of the most beautiful things I had ever heard. The melody line reminded me of a figure skater, gliding over the ice, each high note accented like a jump and twirl into the air. I listened to it over and over, singing along and perfecting each pitch.

I listened, rewound, and listened again. I sang along, immersing myself in the character of Mary Magdalene. Soon I had the words memorized and the melody internalized.

I went in for an audition with Doc and Miss Bobbie. Miss Bobbie played the piano part while I sang the solo. At the end, I sang the last note, a high F, belting it out with all the volume I could muster.

Doc nodded in affirmation. "Do you think you can you hit a high C on that last measure?"

"I think so." Miss Bobbie played it so I could hear it.

"Let's try it."

We backed up a few measures, and I hit the F, and then leaped up to a C. I surprised myself when I hit it. The sound was similar to a dog squeak toy, although slightly more melodic.

"Little thing is standing on her tiptoes!" Miss Bobbie laughed from behind the upright piano.

I didn't realize, but I had popped up on my toes, as if that was going to help me hit the note.

"Will you sing this tomorrow at rehearsal?" Doc asked, smiling.

"Sure!" The idea excited me.

The next night, we rehearsed in the sanctuary. When we got to the duet, Doc signaled a tenor and me to come forward. We walked to the front and removed our microphones from the stands. The tenor offered to share his music, and I shook my head. I wouldn't need it. He seemed surprised.

We began the song, and I started out softly. As the song progressed, I crescendoed through phrases, adding dynamics and emotion. The tenor part began, and we sang our harmonies. Then, the dramatic conclusion started. I put myself in Mary's shoes. I felt her pain, her joy, and elation. I soared through the phrases and hit the high notes with ease. The last note came, and I popped up to the high C as I had rehearsed the day before. I watched Doc for the cutoff; all was silent, the song over.

There was a brief moment of complete silence.

Suddenly I heard a collective "Whoa!" from behind me. The entire choir burst into loud applause. I received pats on the back and compliments the entire way back to my seat.

"Amazing!"

"You have a drop dead gorgeous voice!"

"I don't know if I have the correct musical term, but you ROCKED!"

I beamed at the praise. For all the insecurity I had struggled with through the years, it felt good to land on something I was good at. For so long I had longed to fit in, trying to be good enough for the cool people. All of a sudden I *was* the cool person.

I continued singing solos at church as often as I could. I relished the chance to share the gospel through song.

I hadn't begun to learn guitar yet, so I did the Christian karaoke thing and sang with an accompaniment track. LifeWay and other Christian stores sold CDs and cassettes of popular songs sans vocals. There were shelves and shelves of tracks of instrumental Christian favorites. Classic hymns like "How Great Thou Art" mingled with more popular songs such as "On My Knees" by Jaci Velazquez and "Testify to Love" by Avalon. The instrumentals sounded overly produced, almost robotic in their musicality. Each pitch was faultless, and every chord perfectly in its place. Corny backing vocals emerged for the choruses and faded into *ooos* and *aahs* for the second verse.

I would put those tracks in my cassette player and practice over and over until I perfected the vocal part. Today I cringe when I hear those hokey things, but they were very convenient for a wannabe Christian diva. I loved going to LifeWay and browsing the latest instrumental cassette collection to pick out my next special music.

I loved to sing for Jesus. I was thankful for the ways that He impacted my life. He had given me hope and a newfound confidence. I no longer felt like the gangly teenager trying desperately to fit in. Jesus accepted me as I was and loved me in spite of all my flaws and imperfections. Singing was my way to give back to Him. I sang my heart out for Jesus.

But I would be lying if I said that was the only reason I sang.

Despite my most holy intentions, I got a swelled head. I was a singer, and I was a damn good one. I loved the attention. All eyes were on me. And each time I finished, there were so many words of affirmation. People enjoyed my singing, and I was more than happy to show off for them. The desire to show off wasn't completely bad. I had gained a great amount of self-assurance, and singing in front of people solidified that confidence. Yet, I felt conflicted by this desire and my newfound faith's instructions to be humble.

Special music during church became the time that I could display my vocal talents. I signed up as often as I could, which turned into once every other month. I would have done more, but there were other vocalists that wanted a chance. I'm ashamed to confess that I often felt one of two emotions toward the other singers: pride toward the ones that I was obviously better than and jealousy toward the ones whose talents I felt threatened by.

Singing was a major high for me. I vowed to pursue music for the rest of my life. My profession would be singing for Jesus. In my head, I envisioned the musical career of my future. I would easily sail through my music major and then land some recording contract with a CCM label.

I was about to get a rude awakening as I ventured into my new college major.

8

MY SIMON COWELL MOMENT

I walked into a small lecture room. Several professors sat behind a table with red pens in hand. Some smiled reassuringly; others gave me a look that clearly communicated, "This better be good."

I walked to the pianist and handed him my music. Then, as confidently as I could pretend to be, I walked to center stage.

"Good afternoon. My name is Jamie Rainey, and the first piece I'd like to sing for you is 'A Little China Figure' by Franco Leoni."

The professors nodded, most without looking up from their papers.

I was in the middle of my sophomore year of college when I decided to change my major from Biology to Music. My original career plans had been either an environmentalist or zoologist (I was a bit of a tree hugger in my high school days), but once I had my musical revelation, there was no turning back. The F I received in Organic Chemistry also solidified that decision.

While filling out my application to the Florida State College of Music, I decided on a vocal performance major. I wanted to perform, so it seemed a logical choice.

In that lecture room, my meek soprano voice gave it all it could. There were no microphones. I was expected to project my voice, and it was really hard. I finished with no applause. It felt deafeningly quiet. I maintained composure and kept smiling. After some very awkward silence, one of the professors finally spoke.

"May we hear Brahm's 'Lullaby,' please?"

I nodded and looked to the pianist, who flipped to the music and began to play. I rolled my shoulders back, standing as tall as I could and sang my sloppy German pronunciation. I enjoyed the familiar melody of this piece, but the German was really difficult. I felt much relief when the song ended.

One of the kinder looking professors gave me a weak smile.

"What are your career plans after college?"

I have few moments in my life that I truly regret, words spoken that I wish with all my heart that I could take back. This is one of those moments.

If future me could be in that room, watching college me, I would lunge forward in dramatic slow motion, shouting, "NOOOOOO!!!!" and shove myself to the ground. Whatever it took to stop the next words that were about to come out of my mouth. Even then, in that moment, a small something nudged inside me, urging me not to say it.

And yet, I still said it.

"I want to be a Christian singer-songwriter."

The professor's face noticeably fell. She blinked several times, narrowed her eyes a bit, as if in confusion, and then simply said one word.

"Oh."

I stood my ground and held my smile. The professors mumbled things like, "Using microphones," and "No need to project." They seemed horrified.

The audition ended with some incredibly painful sight-reading. After more awkward silence, the group of professors thanked me, most without ever looking up, and I took the cue to scurry from the room. I escaped that stifling space and almost gasped for air when I closed the door behind me.

Later that day, I received my rejection notice.

I knew the entrance process was strict, and I had prepared myself for a rejection. I was proud of myself for auditioning. It was one of the hardest things I'd ever done.

Declaring my aspiration of being a Christian singer/songwriter seemed like a harmless notion at the time. And yet, I look back on how clueless I was and face palm.

What I didn't realize then was Florida State's Music School is one of the most prestigious in the country. They pride themselves on the fine education they give, and that involves orchestral music and operatic style singing. Something I was not at all interested in at the time.

I had no idea what type of singing they required or that I was doing it all wrong. Singing with a microphone was not what they were going to teach me. They were going to teach me fine vocal quality.

I wasted their time. I stood there and declared my silly notions and grandiose dreams of performing Christian music, and my voice was not what they were looking for in vocal performance. I didn't realize that at the time of the audition. It took several years for that to fully sink in.

It was my own *American Idol* audition moment. My Simon Cowell was a group of operatic vocal professors.

But I was determined to finish my college degree, and I wanted it to be in music. Six months later, I found myself back in that stifling room with those same stoic professors.

I had spent those months studying with a new voice teacher. She was an incredible opera singer, who performed at many community events. I always listened in awe as she sang a phrase and made the windows shake. I tried so hard to mimic it, and yet I always fell short. She remained encouraging and tried countless techniques. I grew frustrated with my pieces. This was not the style of music I wanted to sing. Luckily I'm stubborn, so I pressed on. Things slowly began to click, and my timid voice grew stronger.

She counseled me in the audition process, gently telling me that vocal performance was a very difficult major. I settled on a general Bachelor of Arts in Music. The audition process would not be as intense.

Back in that intimidating audition room, I knew exactly what to do. I handed my music to the accompanist, walked to center stage, and with much more poise than before, introduced myself.

"My name is Jamie Rainey, and my first piece is 'The Lamb' by Theodore Chanler."

As I began to sing, something wasn't right. My voice was really weak.

I know I can sing better than this. What's wrong?

The professors chose the second piece, "Cara e Dolce" by Allessandro Scarlatti, a well-known Italian aria. I launched into it and still didn't feel right. I warmed up today. I had spent months preparing. What was happening?

I was asked the same question from the first audition.

"What are your career plans after college?"

I remembered the look I received the first time I had answered this question. I decided to give a more diplomatic answer.

"I am undecided at this point. I just know I want to do something with music."

That answer was met with approving nods and no weird stares. *Phew.*

I faked my way through some ugly sight-reading and waited anxiously for them to release me.

Eyes downcast at the table in front of them, I heard a deep voice boom out, "Thank you." They were all marking red on their papers.

I couldn't get out of that room fast enough.

I held the tears back until I got to my car. I shut my car door and then let the tears flow. I had blown it. I felt terrible about this audition. There's no way they would accept me. I was so confident that I had bombed that I began to make new college plans. Maybe I would major in religious studies.

Hours later, I returned to the school for a mandatory meeting. I walked toward the doorway and smiled meekly at the guy standing there. He asked for my name. I answered softly and avoided eye contact. My eyes were red and puffy from crying all afternoon.

He looked through a list, put a check by my name, and then shuffled through a stack of envelopes in his other hand. He located the one he was looking for and handed it to me with a smile.

"Congratulations. You made it in."

I stared at him in shock. "Excuse me?"

"You made it in," he repeated. Then with a hushed voice, "You won't need to attend this meeting." Another big smile. "Welcome to the College of Music."

Still smiling, he motioned the envelope towards me again, which I finally took. I stepped outside to the courtyard and sat on a bench. I was oblivious to the cold concrete on my butt and continued to stare at the envelope in my hand. It had my name on it under the Florida State University seal. I slid my finger under the flap and ripped the envelope open.

"Congratulations! We are proud to welcome you into the Florida State College of Music..."

There was more information in the letter, but my mind

couldn't make it past the first line. A mixture of disbelief, excitement, and fear churned through my stomach. It took a few minutes for the disbelief to wear off. The fear slowly subsided, giving full reign to the excitement.

I was going to be a music student.

9

THE STAGE VS. THE HILLTOP

I was in the middle of a Christian mosh pit. It was the summer of 1999, the summer before I began my journey as a music student. Derek and I returned to Creation, but sadly, Travis could not make the trip this time. I was sad that our trio was incomplete.

We picked up two new willing travelers: Shyam and my boyfriend Tim. Tim was not a Christian, and I was praying hard for a dramatic conversion.

We decided against renting the death-mobile from Lucky's Rent-a-Car. Somehow, we talked Derek's dad into letting us take his brand new minivan. His father is much kinder than I am. I doubt I would let a group of road-trip-crazy, college kids take my new minivan five states away. For whatever reason, he did, and we traveled in style that year. We also had a lot more legroom.

We arrived at Creation and set up camp. It was similar to the previous year with our circle of little tents and my dad's Coleman stove. I pulled my Bible out of my bag and set it by my pillow. I was ready for a week of spiritual filling.

The week was filled with lots of concerts, inspiring speakers, and icy cold showers that I simply refused to take. In between concerts, we relaxed at the campsite, having deep conversations about life. I kept giving Tim the side eye to see if the numerous altar calls he had witnessed were having any effect on him. After almost every concert, each band would stand center stage and declare that God was calling out to someone, wanting to be let into their heart. The lead singer would urge that person (or group of people) to let go and let God in. With eyes closed all across that large field, the singer would say, "If you are feeling God tug on your heart, please raise your hand. We want to pray for you."

I would crack one eye open and look toward Tim. Each and every altar call, he sat quietly, eyes closed, head bowed, hands folded in his lap.

Dang it.

He seemed to enjoy the concerts. He clapped along and smiled as he watched me sway to the music and sing along to every lyric. He particularly enjoyed Third Day, so I made a mental note to play more of their albums while around him.

But he was not budging on those altar calls. I was disappointed, but it only made me pray harder for his salvation.

On one of the last nights, we picked a spot close to the front. The evening was winding to a close, and the more popular bands were hitting the stage. Our spot had been relatively empty the rest of the day, but now people were crowding around for the final concert.

If I went to Creation now, I'd be one of the people in the shade at the back of the field, sipping ice water in my comfy lawn chair. Nineteen-year-old me had a lot more energy, and music fueled it. When those bands started, no amount of exhaustion could keep me down.

And yet, even with the drive from the music, my energy was waning. I was tired from bouncing around in the summer heat. It was getting late, and although it had been a great week, it had also been a long week. My back hurt from sleeping on a lumpy air mattress, and I was tired of smelling funny. I was thankful for the spiritual renewing but more than ready for a hot shower and clean sheets.

I threw a hand over my mouth as a yawn took over my entire face. I mustered up some energy for the last show.

As Jars of Clay took the stage, bright lights bounced across the trees surrounding us, and loud guitars rattled my eardrums. People jumped as the energy from the stage roared and grew louder. The crowd became unaware of the people around them, and soon I was being run into and almost shoved over without an apology.

Strangers screamed in my ears. I huddled close to my friends, and being the gentlemen they were, they tried to shield me from the crowd. Tim was especially protective, trying in vain to protect his girl. Despite their efforts, they were simply shoved into me as the mosh pit crowd lunged to and fro.

"Ooof..." I heard Derek mutter as his elbow accidentally jabbed me in the side. We glared at the people around us, but they were too lost in the concert experience to even notice.

Water came flying down from the sky, likely from a water bottle someone was flinging about. Droplets showered over us, and I felt a few drops peg me directly in the eyeball. I jolted from the shock and wiped my now stinging eye. Shyam let out a loud, "HEY!," but it fell silent amidst all the noise surrounding us.

This is a CHRISTIAN concert? I was ready to join 40-year-old me in the lawn chair.

The show wound to a close, and I walked away disappointed. The atmosphere had made the concert impossible to enjoy. I couldn't shake the feeling that the people I had just been around had not been very Christ-like. I sighed and shook my head.

We were walking back toward our campsite, anticipating

bedtime. That lumpy air mattress was sounding pretty good. Then I looked to the left. Perched atop a hill were thirteen wooden crosses.

"Hey guys," I stopped and pointed. "I'd like to go see them."

Derek was exhausted and decided to return to camp. I didn't blame him, but this was my last chance to see the crosses. Shyam and Tim were willing, so the three of us slowly trekked up the hill.

Several months prior, the nation had been rocked by the Columbine High School shootings. The news had been ablaze with the stories from that horrendous day, and the Christian church was proudly telling the stories of brave students like Cassie Bernall and Rachel Scott. With a gun to their head, these two young women allegedly refused to deny God. They were both killed. The Christian church raised them up as examples of the martyrs we should all be willing to be. We'd been hearing their stories all week.

A man had built 13 crosses in memory of the Columbine victims. These crosses had traveled around the country to different Christian concerts and events. They were made of simple wood and were built to remember each teacher and student that died that day.

After climbing the hill, we encountered a silent crowd. We fell in line and waited our turn. As we approached each cross, I noticed a name, short biography, and a picture. Different colored Sharpies had covered the crosses in Bible verses, messages, and prayers. Crosses and necklaces were strapped to each one. Some even left a teddy bear offering at the foot of a few.

As we walked by each cross, I noticed that no one was shoving anyone to get a better look. In fact, if someone was peering to see better, the person in front of them kindly stepped out of the way to allow them more space. People held flashlights up so that others could read the messages in the pitch-black night.

I walked from cross to cross, pausing at each one and trailing my fingers across the grain of the wood. I squinted to read the messages scribbled in the pale moonlight and smiled as a flashlight beam lightened my view. My fingers ran through a strand of plastic beads that quietly tinkled as they fell against the wood. Kneeling in front of the last, I softly stroked the cheek of the teddy bear leaning at the foot of the cross.

Then the singing started.

I don't know how it started. I don't know who started it. It's as if the crowd just began in unison, all softly singing together. As we walked and solemnly stood at the foot of each cross, we softly sang praise songs and hymns. "Awesome God." "Amazing Grace." Tears were shed. Prayers were prayed.

We worshipped.

On that peaceful hilltop, I found a worship I didn't realize existed. I was so moved that I cried heavy tears, my body wracked by sobs.

I knew the horror of what had happened at Columbine, but it didn't fully sink in until the hilltop. It was one of the first major tragedies that occurred in my lifetime, and it affected me deeply. I am intensely sensitive and severely impacted by sorrow. This was my first real taste of feeling the pain of that grief. I cried for the young lives that had been lost, teenagers that would never realize their full potential. I sobbed for the families that would never hug them again. I wept for the gunmen, two young men that clearly needed the love of Jesus.

But beyond the grief, I was struck by the beauty of human nature that was unfolding before me. Witnessing the kindness that strangers extended to each other in offering the glow of their flashlights was touching. And then to hear everyone softly sing together, sharing in this moment, carving out a tiny piece of love and beauty in the midst of the horrors of our world. We were united together through our love of Jesus. I cried from sadness but also from the hope felt through those melodies that drifted through the air.

It was time for the crosses to continue to their next destination. They were gently pulled out of the ground, passed along the top of the crowd, and loaded onto a truck. No pushing. No fighting. The mass of people worked together, gently crowd surfing the crosses onto the truck.

As we watched the crosses be passed over the heads of the crowd, we stopped for a moment and listened to the singing. Tears once again pricked my eyes and slowly ran down my cheek. The crowd continued to softly sing behind us. After a few moments, the three of us walked to the edge of the hill and sat. Leaning against each other, we perched and enjoyed the quiet of the night.

PART IV

SYNCOPATION

10

MEDIOCRE MUSIC

On my first official day as a music major, I entered the campus with much trepidation. The excitement I had felt upon learning of my acceptance into the school had slowly worn away, and the fear had now taken full control. Declaring myself a musician was a big step, and I was terrified that someone would tell me I wasn't good enough. I watched the confident masters students stroll past. I clutched my newly-purchased books close to myself, hoping they would block people from seeing my heart practically pounding out of my chest. I felt like I was back in middle school.

I walked toward my new voice teacher's studio. I could feel sweat drenching the armpits of my shirt. I looked at the nameplate on the door: Dr. David Wingate. I knocked and heard a big booming voice echo from inside.

"Come in!"

I entered the room and saw an older, bearded man sitting in a desk chair. He swiveled around and looked at me from head to toe. Was he sizing me up? He turned and looked at a paper on his desk.

"Jamie?"

"Yes."

He motioned toward a leather couch. I perched on the edge, trying to appear poised. Real singers are poised.

"Tell me about yourself."

I hate this question. Where do you start? With birth? My brain raced, and I settled on a short musical background of myself. Surely that's all he cared about.

I explained how I had just switched majors from science to music. His eyebrows rose. I couldn't tell if that was a good thing. Most people were surprised when they heard of my drastic major change, but something about his reaction intimidated me.

"How many years have you been studying voice?" he asked after a few moments of silence.

I swallowed hard. "Um... I've only taken lessons for the last year." I saw the eyebrows rise again, and I quickly offered, "But I've been singing in choirs for years!"

"Mmm hmm..." He looked back at the paper on his desk. I looked down at my folded hands in my lap.

"Well, let's see what you got." He gingerly pushed himself up from his office chair and hobbled over toward the piano, leaning heavily on a wooden cane. I learned later that he had suffered a stroke and that semester was his first one back teaching.

I stood up and walked closer to the baby grand sitting by the window. I wasn't sure where to stand. He looked up and motioned toward a spot on the floor. I hurried to it and looked at the ground, hoping he couldn't see my face flushing.

As he began playing scales and singing exercises that I was to imitate, I ran through all the vocal techniques that I had learned through the years. Stand up straight, shoulders back, inhale the breath like through a straw. Despite all my efforts to sound confident, the waver in my voice gave me away.

He watched every move I made. I could feel his eyes on my slouched shoulders, and I tried my best to keep them high.

"Hmmm."

I wanted to melt into the puddle of sweat that must have been gathering under me.

I tried desperately to look confident, but my nervous laughter kept giving me away. He began yet another scale, pounding it on the keyboard while eyeing me with a raised eyebrow.

"Keep your shoulders back."

I just told myself to do that very thing. I was trying hard to stand tall, but I felt so little standing before him that my shoulders instinctively pulled forward. I was practically cowering before him.

"Use the breath to power the phrase!" he thundered so loudly I jumped a bit. To say he was intimidating was an understatement. I tried to breathe deep, to fill up like a balloon and slowly and powerfully release that breath through each phrase. My nerves were making my breath so shallow.

More scales.

"Round the vowel."

I thought I was! I grew discouraged that the things that I thought I knew so well were not being done properly before this new teacher.

"Louder."

My meek voice cracked slightly as I raised the volume. *Yikes.* He looked at me over his glasses, obviously disapproving of the quiet volume I produced.

"You need more breath support. Fill up your diaphragm."

I'm trying... Is this darn lesson done yet? I tried to concentrate on that elusive stomach muscle that singers are so obsessed with.

As the first lesson finally wound to a close, I tried not to act too excited as I darted out of there.

The semester didn't get much better after that.

I liked my voice teacher. He was fun and had great stories. I smiled as he told me about his wife of forty years. "We've never once considered divorce!" he proudly told me one day. "Murder a couple times, but never divorce!" It was the first time I had heard that old joke, and I laughed.

As the weeks went on I began to relax around him. I appreciated his attempt to lighten the mood. Still, fun stories didn't help my vocal technique. He tried everything he could think of, but his visual pictures didn't click. I just couldn't seem to make my voice into what he wanted it to be: a big booming vibrato, a full and blossoming brightness circling through the air and effortlessly floating toward the ears of the listeners. I knew that he wanted me to sing like every stereotypical opera singer (I threw a Viking helmet onto the head of my visual image) – big, dramatic, and loud.

I grew bored with his song selections. Opera arias were not my performance goal. I learned quickly how this school frowned upon contemporary-style singing. I longed to sing the songs I sang at church. These classical pieces were killing me, one adagio passage at a time.

I spent hours on the Baroque pieces Dr. Wingate assigned. I wanted so much to do something right and see him smile. I tried to learn "Oh Sleep, Why Dost Thou Leave Me?" by Handel. The melody was pretty, but I couldn't get the melismas. Measure after painful measure, there were long phrases with dozens of quick sixteenth notes strung together. The goal was to beautifully connect these notes together in one effortless phrase. No matter how much I practiced those runs, I never got any better. My recreation of them was always sloppy, and the rhythm was never right. The notes moved too quickly for my voice to properly sing them. "I Attempt From Love's Sickness" by Henry Purcell was a bit easier to sing. However, my apathy toward the song was more than evident in my execution.

In the middle of one particularly grueling lesson, Dr. Wingate took a deep breath and paused. He gazed out the small window of his office door. He stroked his beard for a moment and then looked at me. I looked down at the music stand, desperately hoping that the notes on the page would sink into my subconscious and then flow out of my vocal cords with ease. Afraid to meet his gaze, I bit my lip and continued to stare at the stanzas in front of me, pretending to scribble notes in the margins. We'd spent half the lesson working on one of those Baroque pieces with no breakthrough. He decided to change the subject.

"You sing in your church choir, right?"

"Yes." I shifted uncomfortably on my feet.

"Are you doing anything special for Christmas?"

"Yes... We're working on a cantata."

"Are you doing any solos?"

"Yes!" I finally met his gaze. "I have two solos." I had been listening to the rehearsal tape for weeks, diligently practicing.

"Why don't you bring those in next week? I'd like to hear them."

I broke into a big smile. Anything to get away from the "Nymphs and Shepherds" song I had been trudging through for weeks.

The following week, I brought the cantata music. My accompanist played the intro, and I passionately sang. It felt good to sing a song to God instead of a silly opera aria. I finished to the sound of no applause. I was getting used to that around this place.

He made a slight nod of approval. "Your voice certainly blossoms with a song you connect with."

See! I thought. I knew I didn't totally suck.

Then he frowned.

Uh oh.

"What bothers me is how churches are performing this mediocre music."

My heart fell. Mediocre music? What?

That statement crushed me. I wanted to snatch my music off the stand and shout in his face, "FINE! I'll take my crappy music and go sing for someone who appreciates it!"

But I didn't. He possessed the power to help me through this, and I needed to trust him. I still needed to pass my vocal jury. A jury was like the initial audition process: you performed several pieces in front of the vocal faculty, and they judged you on your ability. They also decided if you were good enough to go onto the next grade. As much as I was not enjoying this particular kind of vocal training, I loved the other areas of my music study. My music theory classes had been invaluable, and I knew those classes, along with others I had yet to take, would only help to improve my musicality. I did not want to be kicked out because I wasn't singing the way they expected. It was frustrating, but I knew that Dr. Wingate possessed the knowledge to help me pass that jury and to continue in my music studies.

So we put my mediocre music aside and went back to Henry Purcell.

Dr. Wingate offended me that day, but years later I would completely understand his declaration. In his world of Bach cantatas and Mozart requiems, that little church cantata didn't even come close. And it couldn't. It's kind of unfair to compare the two.

When you take the time to really dig into classical music, the complexities in the phrases are astounding. While studying music history, I was blown away by the story of Bach. He was hired as a church musician and performed a cantata each week. Each piece included a full choir, a boy's choir, and an orchestra. The choir parts are crazy difficult, with each part entering at different times and singing complex patterns and rounds. He often composed a new piece each week. The fact that he could piece together a work that intricate, and so many of them, is amazing to me.

The church Christmas cantata was simpler, basic chords and melodies with easy to sing choir parts. I cannot recall the name of that cantata or the title of my solos. The melodies have long since left my brain. I'm sure the composer worked very hard, and I couldn't come close to putting together a work of that magnitude.

I understand how inaccessible classical music is to many people. When I began my study as a music student, I didn't understand it at all. Growing up, I would tolerate the Strauss waltzes that my mother loved, but wouldn't listen to much classical music beyond that. After years of study, I began to understand, respect, and love it.

And although I now understand (and even agree with) Dr. Wingate's statement, I do want to avoid falling into the pitfall of being overly critical. I grew weary of the constant music snobbery that surrounded me at Florida State. Any music that wasn't done in a classical style was considered lesser or not good enough. I believe there is beauty to be found in all music, no matter how simplistic we may think it.

I don't believe all "mediocre music" (as Dr. Wingate would define it) is bad. Sometimes simplicity is perfect. I think of the scene in *Mr. Holland's Opus*, where he tries to reach the young clarinet player who is so desperate to be good at music, to be good at anything. I related to that character so much.

As she brushes away her tears, Mr. Holland pulls out a record player and plays a popular hit. He makes a reference to the simple chord structure and repetitive melody. Then he says, "But I like it. You know why?"

She looks at him through tear stained eyes. "Why?"

"Because it's fun."

He reminds her that music should be fun. Some simple songs are simply fun. They communicate much with so little.

Music doesn't have to be complex to be meaningful. Simplistic songs do not necessarily equal bad songs. Just because a song only has three chords doesn't make it poor quality. Sometimes simple speaks more than an intensely-crafted symphony. There are days where my heart is heavy, my body weary, and my mind tired. A simple song with an easy melody can empower.

But had I stayed at simple, I would have missed out on so much. I almost missed the beauty of Mozart and Bach and Beethoven and Franz Liszt because I was so preoccupied with the three-chord, one-hit wonders on Christian radio.

Most of the contemporary Christian music I longed to sing fell under that mediocre music category. While fighting through my first year of voice lessons, I just wanted to go back to the easier music. But had I stayed with that easier music, I never would have stretched, never would have grown, and never would have known the joy of seeing what long, hard months of practice could cause my voice to produce.

As I moved to a new voice teacher (Dr. Wingate and I finally decided things just weren't working out and came to the mutual decision that it would be best if I studied with a different teacher), I continued to push myself over the next two and a half years of lessons. Under the tutelage of my new teacher, Mrs. Ford, I amazed myself at the sounds that emerged from my vocal cords. My tone was more focused, my volume louder, my breath support stronger. And, not surprisingly, my self-confidence improved. I passed not just one, but three juries. The vocal faculty continued to let me progress onto the next year of study, so I obviously did something right.

The more I studied classical music, and even those silly opera arias, the more my appreciation grew. My understanding of musical structure developed and my ear began to hear and recognize intervals. I found myself singing difficult songs and phrases that I never thought I could.

In my final year as a music student, I performed a recital of sacred songs. For months I perfected ten pieces, singing them over and over and over in the cramped practice rooms. One spring afternoon I locked myself into my favorite room, tucked away in the back of the hallway. I hit my pitch on the slightly out of tune upright pianos and then powerfully sang through "O Vos Omnes" by Theodore Dubois. For the last three years, I had sat in those practice rooms listening to the vocal powerhouses in the surrounding practice rooms, feeling intimidated. I no longer felt intimidated. I had finally found my voice, and I was so proud of it.

As much as I never thought I would admit it, I miss those difficult pieces I used to perform, those demanding melodies that required hours of practice and work. I am thankful for the incredibly challenging classical pieces, for the long vocal runs littered with sixteenth notes, for the soaring high notes that caused me to practically squeeze my diaphragm out of my body. I needed to see what I was capable of with a lot of really hard work. That discipline has stuck with me and shown me that I am able to do more than I think, even beyond music.

I spent hours perfecting pitch and getting tone just right. Those songs made me work harder than I ever had before, vocally and in general. The songs I would sing for church were simpler. I learned, memorized, and perfected them in just a couple days. I grew lazy with those pieces. They didn't challenge me. I needed the challenge of classical music to show myself what I was really capable of.

My teacher's question continued to echo in my brain for years to come. Even after receiving my music degree, it lingered.

Why *are* churches performing this mediocre music?

11

THE EVILS OF PINK FLOYD

Missionary dating is not a good idea. And yet I still tried it. Tim was my college sweetheart. He was not a Christian despite my desperate prayers for God to make him into one. He was well aware of my attempts, including each and every altar call I had hoped he would respond to at Creation. I'm surprised he didn't run screaming.

We met in chemistry lab when I was still a Biology major. We sat at the same table and ended up lab partners, measuring beakers of solution into test tubes together. We had an inside joke that it was his sexy safety goggles that made me weak in the knees.

Tim was kind, gracious, and incredibly smart. I remember first being attracted to his big smile. Before we ever dated, we would have deep conversations about the meaning of life and the existence of God. I was impressed at his thoughtful answers and his willingness to be vulnerable. He wasn't afraid to be honest with me, even regarding his faith or lack thereof.

I knew he wasn't a Christian. I also knew that for that reason I probably shouldn't date him. I knew that I wanted to marry a Christian, so it made sense to date someone who was one. Or to not date someone who wasn't. But Tim swept me off my feet, and when he officially asked me to be his girlfriend, I couldn't say no. Plus, I figured getting closer to him would be a good way to share more of Jesus with him. Tim was the first agnostic I had ever met. I took agnostic to mean, "I haven't yet been convinced of how I need Jesus." Challenge accepted.

We had a great relationship. He was proud of me for pursuing music and constantly encouraged me. Tim had always loved music. After I was accepted into the College of Music, he became more serious about learning piano. He had taken some lessons as a child, but as life had gotten busier, he had stopped. Inspired by my music studies, he bought a set of piano books and began to teach himself. He diligently worked his way through each level. He was so excited when he began to play "In the Hall of the Mountain King" by Edward Grieg. After weeks of practicing, he proudly played it for me. I was impressed at how much he had learned in a few short weeks.

Part of my music curriculum was going to 15 recitals each semester. I dragged Tim along to more concerts than I can count. He enjoyed most of them, being a fan of classical music. But there were a few weird ones; "New Music" compositions that I crammed in at the last minute to get the last few recital credits I needed. We both stifled back giggles through the recital where the flutist shouted into her instrument and a pianist stuffed metal nuts and bolts into the strings to achieve a new kind of sound. We knew it wasn't meant to be comical, but it was hard to choke down the laughter.

Tim and I laughed a lot. He had a great sense of humor, and I always giggled at his jokes. Along with laughter, deep conversations filled many of our evenings together. As long as we weren't engaging in some religious discussion where I became emotionally wrought at his soul's eternal damnation, things were great.

I was so desperate to save him that I became manipulative.

Since Christian music had impacted me so much, I was certain that it would be the doorway to his salvation too. So I played it around him. Constantly.

He was gracious. He could have easily commented on the lack of lyrical originality or the simplistic chord structure. He never did. He listened to each and every band I played. He went to not one but two Christian music festivals with me. That boy must have really loved me.

I listened to some of his music too. He played a generous amount of classical music around me. Now that I was studying it, I was able to do more than simply endure it. He introduced me to Franz Liszt, one of the most amazing piano composers of all time. I still love his piano sonatas.

He also exposed me to Billy Joel, his favorite musician. Although I didn't care for some of his atheistic lyrics, I had to admit I liked his music. We even adopted one of his songs as "our" song. "For the Longest Time" still makes me smile.

He crossed the line when he gave me a Pink Floyd album. I was already pushing it with Billy Joel. I had ventured out of my Christian bubble for that. Wasn't that enough?

"*Dark Side of the Moon* is one of my favorite albums. There are these beautifully cryptic lyrics woven throughout. I think you'll really like it."

I looked at the dark cover. There was some triangular prism looking thing with a rainbow flowing out of one side. I was pretty sure Satan drew the album art himself.

I tentatively took the album. "I'll try it."

I took it home and played it. I remember electric guitars and drums, the usual assortment of instruments. Then I heard it.

Shit.

The word was an insult to my very soul. I flew over to my CD player and hit stop. Since accepting Christ, profanity had become one of my number one no-nos. No longer was I the sixteen year old throwing inhibition to the wind and shouting along with Nine Inch Nails. I couldn't allow this filth to fill my ears.

I returned the album to Tim.

"I can't listen to this."

"Wh...what? Why not?"

"There's bad language in it," I gave him a disapproving look that clearly stated, "Why are *you* listening to this?"

He was dumbfounded.

"If you can get past that, it's a really powerful album! I really think you'll like it!"

"No, thank you," I refused. With my arms crossed in front of me, I refused to come off my holy high horse.

I could tell he was shocked and a little peeved. He narrowed his eyebrows, and he seemed like he was about to say something. The jewel case that he held in his hand slowly fell to his side.

Then his shoulders slumped forward. He sighed and simply said, "Okay."

He put the CD back into his collection and never pushed the issue again.

I can't express how ashamed I am of that moment. I had spent months cramming Christian music down his throat. He had graciously listened, although I am sure he was ready to crack some of those CDs in half. Then he opened up his musical world to me, an incredibly important part of his life, and I rejected it.

Years later, my pastor helped me realize how sheltered my music life had become. She mentioned a couple secular albums and artists, and I returned the statement with a blank stare and a blink.

"You haven't listened to them?"

I had barely even heard of them, let alone listened to them.

She gave me a disapproving yet gentle and concerned look.

"Jamie, you really ought to branch out a bit in your music listening."

I sheepishly looked at my feet and nodded. I knew she was right. But Christian music was safe, and I was nervous about branching out into unknown territory. I thought of the insecurities from middle and high school. When I listened to Christian music, I felt more confidence. I knew that Jesus accepted and loved me. Outside of that I wasn't so sure. I was also afraid of being corrupted by secular music. My faith had taught me to be in the world but not of it, and I had tried hard to obey that, limiting all of my interactions with things that weren't safely labeled Christian.

I stayed sheltered for so long because my life situation remained the same. Since I lived at home for college, my college years just felt like an extension of high school. I didn't have the experience of living in a dorm, meeting a new roommate from states away with a different worldview. I did meet new friends through classes but didn't make many efforts to hang out with them outside of class. Each night as I finished classes, I drove home and returned to the room that I had lived in for ten years: same dcTalk poster on the wall, same albums in my CD player. On the weekends, I went to the same church that I had attended for ten years. Much of my life stayed the same, and I didn't see a reason to change much or to challenge myself.

If Tim were to hand me that Pink Floyd album now, I would listen to it in its entirety, and the word *shit* wouldn't make me bat an eye. I would take in all the lyrical depth and consider the music and the talent of the musicians. I would be impacted by the album's passion.

I have listened to *The Dark Side of the Moon* since. I can honestly say it's not my favorite album, mainly because classic rock is just not my style of music. But if I had it to do over again, I would at least do him the honor of giving the album a chance.

There is beauty and passion to be found in all music. I was too stubborn and close-minded to even give it a full listen. And the more I've heard the songs from *Dark Side of the Moon*, the more it grows on me. I can now see why Tim was eager to share it with me. I understand why the album was, and still is, such a big deal.

I recently heard a version of "Stairway to Heaven" and was blown away by the power and intensity of the music. It was the first time I had ever listened to the song in its entirety. Much like Pink Floyd, I shunned Led Zeppelin. I avoided that song for years because I thought it was evil.

I hate that I have missed out on some amazing music. For years I believed that if music wasn't specifically about God it wasn't worth listening to. I limited myself to only Christian music. Surely truly impassioned music could only be about our Lord.

Tim is one of the most gracious people I have ever met. Although he held tight to his agnostic beliefs, he treated me with more love and respect than most Christians I know. We eventually parted ways after we realized that neither of us was going to budge in our beliefs. I finally let go of the notion that I had to stay with him and bring him to Christ.

We broke up on good terms and remained friends. I met his girlfriend (who soon became his wife) and loved her. When I got married, Tim was there, grinning at me as I walked down the aisle.

As I was writing the first draft of this book, I e-mailed him an apology for shoving Jesus down his throat. He responded with the same grace and respect. He knew I was always genuine, and he respected me for my intense faith. In the same way, I respect him for not buying into Christianity simply for the sake of his Jesus-Freak girlfriend.

12

NOISY WORSHIP

Squinting a bit, I looked out at the crowd. It seemed a lot of people had shown up for worship, but I couldn't really tell. The lights were really bright.

I took deep breaths to untie the knots in my stomach. I had only been leading worship for a few weeks. I wondered if I would ever get over the pre-service butterflies. My hands were clammy, and I was worried the microphone would slip from my grasp. I wiped my sweaty palm against my skirt. I swallowed hard and peered out again into the sea of people. The blinding spotlight once again prevented me from seeing much.

The music started. I held the microphone to my lips and began to sing. From what I could see of the crowd, they seemed disengaged.

I must be boring them. I should step it up a bit.

We came to an "I sing, you sing" part, where the congregation echoed the worship leader. I sang my part and then held the microphone out to the crowd. I had seen a hundred Christian musicians do it in concert. It worked every time.

It didn't work. My hand hung limply in front of me while I

heard a half-heartedly-sung phrase drift up to the stage. I swear I heard crickets.

The song finished, and the band began the next. It was another upbeat ballad to our Savior. Raising my hands over my head, I made the motion of hands clapping. I accidentally thumped the microphone, and I grimaced at the *thwack* that emerged from my monitor. I did see a few people begin to clap, so at least that worked... for about eight measures. As I brought the microphone back to my lips, I watched the few people I could see clap and then slowly, one by one, stop. Each person would clap for a bit, then look to his or her neighbor. They would awkwardly clap for a couple more measures and then bring their hands back down to their sides.

I tried to bring the energy in the room back up, smiling big and swaying a bit to the music as it played behind me. I put the microphone into the stand so I could once again lead the congregation in clapping. My hands soon tired from holding them overhead, and the stand prevented me from clapping in front of my body. I gave up and just held the microphone.

There was a short instrumental interlude halfway through the song, and I stood awkwardly as the guitarists played. I felt that I should say something, fill the gap with some words. I thought of all the CCM bands I had seen and thought that I should be shouting out a "Praise Jesus!" or maybe a "Hallelujah!" I opened my mouth to say something, but the words wouldn't come. I could not seem to make my vocal cords do anything beyond the melodies of the songs we sang. I decided that the next week I should prepare a Scripture to fill any voids.

The energetic songs wrapped up, and we moved into a couple slower, more contemplative songs. I relaxed a bit and felt a little more in my element. I closed my eyes tight and let the melodies sweep me away.

Two songs later and the worship set was over. I exhaled and stepped off the stage. I was slightly disappointed in how I had done. I made a mental note to try harder next week. I needed to draw the congregation in more fully to worship, needed to create an energetic atmosphere where the joy of Christ could flow freely. That would probably involve lots of animated shouting into the microphone, clapping, and hyping the audience.

All I knew of worship leading I learned from contemporary Christian music.

That was the knowledge I carried with me when I accepted a part-time worship leader position at my church. I was fresh out of college with my music degree in hand. I had decided to pursue the church music program at Florida State. I quickly found that my Hymnology and Sacred Solo Vocal Literature classes didn't help me much with contemporary worship. So, I relied on the many CCM concerts I had attended over the years.

I still had dreams of becoming a CCM singer-songwriter, but I wasn't sure how to pursue it. I felt more confident in my musicality. Sticking it out at Florida State now felt well worth it. I understood a great deal more music theory, and my voice was so much stronger. And yet, those college classes had not helped move me toward my career choice of contemporary Christian musician. I needed a job, so when my church offered me a part-time worship leader position, I gladly accepted.

Since I had no idea what I was doing, I decided to follow all the other worship leaders I had seen through the years. They were big and flamboyant, hands raised high to the heavens and shouting out instructions or inspiring Bible verses.

I tried to do these things when I led, but I couldn't seem to break out of my shy shell. I figured it would come with time and practice. It had taken years to fully form my voice at Florida State, so surely effective worship leading would take time.

Those first few weeks were scary. I kept the expectation of

loud, energetic worship in my head. Voids of silence should be filled with encouraging words or memorized Scripture. In my mind, that was the only way to lead. It was really the only way I had seen.

I felt awkward as I stood on stage with all eyes on me. Even though I had sung special music at church for years, worship leading felt different. With special music, I could just bring my song as an offering. I felt like it was only Jesus and me. With worship leading, there was an expectation. I was expected to bring the audience into my musical offering with me, and I was having a really hard time with that.

I wished I were a little more skilled at guitar so I could have something to hide behind. I had been teaching myself for about a year (working out of a *Guitar for Dummies* book) but was not ready to play in front of people. Now I wished I had spent more time practicing. Playing guitar would also give me something to do with my hands. I fiddled with the microphone cord each week instead.

Week after week, I tried to fit myself into the mold of the energetic worship leader. And week after week, I completely failed. I looked out and only saw apathetic faces, bored expressions, and listless worshippers shifting uncomfortably on their feet. It was nothing like the crowds I had worshipped in in the past; hands raised high, eyes closed tight with tears sliding down each cheek. I was desperate to create that atmosphere, but I had no idea how.

One night after rehearsal I stayed behind to turn off the lights and lock up the building. The rest of the band had left, and I picked up the last of the chord charts from their music stands. As I gathered my things in the darkness, I looked out at the sea of empty chairs. A huge sigh escaped my lungs. I felt a few tears prick my eyes. I dropped my three-ring binder stuffed with worship choruses. My knees hit the floor.

"God, " I said into the emptiness, "Please. Help me."

The fellowship hall remained silent.

"I don't know what I'm doing. Can You give me a hand? A voice? Some energy?"

More silence. Another sigh escaped from my lungs.

"I want to serve these people. I want to help lead them into worship and be awed in Your presence. But I'm doing it all wrong."

I looked down at my hands, which were wringing themselves nervously. I looked out at the sea of chairs again, which still didn't offer any answers.

"Please. Help me."

I rose to my feet and gathered my things. The door clanged loudly behind me as I left the empty space.

I didn't get any answers that night. I didn't hear God's still, small voice say something encouraging like, "My child, you are enough." Despite the lack of answers, that desperate prayer gave me the courage to keep trying. And through the next few months of trying, I also came to realize that I wasn't doing it all wrong.

I never mastered the art of energetic worship leading. Instead, I learned to be okay with the unique way I led. It wasn't loud or powerful; instead, I led in a quiet, unassuming way. Rather than having insightful words to fill the silence, I learned to be okay with the quiet. I sang as best as I could and then got out of the way. I still wasn't able to create that energetic atmosphere with a sea of hands in the air, but I finally saw past the bored faces. In the faces of others, I saw a gentle peace, a bit of hope. Their hands were often at their sides or clutched in front of their waist rather than held high. But there was a slight smile that tugged at their lips. They weren't jumping, but they were engaged.

As I've come to grips with my disillusionment of Christian subculture, I realized worship leading was one of the biggest. I was under the assumption that worship leading could only be done one way: big and loud. When I failed to produce that, I felt like a failure.

It took me a long time to be okay with myself as a worship leader and even as a worshiper. There is no one-way to lead worship. There's no formula. It's okay to jump up and down and express excitement. It's also okay to sit quietly and contemplate the vastness of God

After a year of worship leading, I finally felt comfortable on the stage, behind the microphone. By then, it was time to begin a new adventure.

PART V

KEY CHANGE

13

THE MOST BEAUTIFUL SOUND

A year and a half after college graduation, I was on a plane flying across the ocean. After a long and frightful trip by myself, I landed in Uganda. I got through customs, claimed my large bags, and met the kind strangers that were picking me up. I was tired, scared, and excited.

We made conversation on the way to the choir-training facility, but mostly I stared out the window, taking it all in. It wasn't my first trip out of the country. I had traveled to Ecuador the previous year to visit my sponsored Compassion child. The two countries seemed similar. Dusty streets, crazy drivers weaving in and out of traffic, and lots of pedestrians with loads that seemed too much atop their heads. I saw children taking baths in plastic buckets out by the road and storefronts busy with customers. My jet-lagged brain struggled to take it all in.

I was here to work with the African Children's Choir. I had seen them perform ten months ago, and they needed volunteers to travel with the children. I jumped at the opportunity. For years, I had had a passion for mission work. When my ideal job of a contemporary Christian musician didn't come to fruition, I dreamed of being a missionary. When I heard of an opportunity to be a music teacher to a choir of African children, I couldn't believe how perfect it sounded. Plus, it involved traveling. I had been bit by the traveling bug and was anxious to explore new places. Since I was fresh out of college with no major commitments, it seemed like an opportunity straight from God.

We arrived at the house where my journey with the choir began. A whir of children raced out of the house and zealously greeted me.

"Welcome Auntie!" the little voices declared. Auntie would be my new title. Tiny arms wrapped around me, and eager faces looked up at me with bright smiles. I was drowning in cuteness.

A handful of other chaperones followed the children, offering warm hugs and help with my luggage. I met Emily, who greeted me with the same welcome I received from the kids.

"Welcome Auntie!" she said with a big grin. I remembered Emily from a training weekend in the States several months before. I liked her immediately. We soon became best friends.

I received a snack of a hard-boiled egg and a small banana. The other adults understood that I was tired and overwhelmed. They escorted me upstairs to the room I would share with two others. They shut the door behind me, inviting me back downstairs when I was ready. I was thankful for a little time to process. My head was spinning.

I looked around at my home for the next two weeks. There were three beds in the room. One single bed sat against the far left wall, and the bunk beds directly in front of me sat against the window. Mosquito netting covered all three. I learned later that one of the locals called the beds "princess beds." She saw the mosquito netting as some sort of royal bedchamber.

The open window let in a small breeze that blew the thin

curtain up slightly. The room was warm so the breeze was welcome. I could hear the sounds of Kampala traffic in the background.

The room was simple, with its concrete floor and modest metal beds, but my heart sighed happily. I was glad for a homey little place. I thanked God once again that I was here.

I was grimy and sweaty from two days of traveling, but unfortunately had no option for the bath I so desperately wanted. There was indoor plumbing and even a bathtub, but I learned that the water would cut off at random times. The electricity often did the same. I rifled around in my bag and pulled out some hand sanitizer, contenting myself with a quick antibacterial gel bath until the water came back.

I hoisted myself up into the top bunk (being the last to arrive, I got whatever was left) to try and get a little bit of rest. This proved difficult, as it was 10:00 in the morning and the sun was streaming through the window, right in my face. I comforted myself by simply lying down. Being horizontal felt glorious. I took some deep breaths and tried to convince myself that I really was in Africa. I put my headphones on and slipped in Shane & Shane's "Carry Away," one of my favorite Christian CDs, to calm my soul.

As I lay there, another sound began to drown out the music on my CD. I slipped the earphones off and listened.

One of the most beautiful sounds I have ever heard drifted its way through the open window by my head. Haunting melodies in a strange tongue intertwined with lively drumbeats, laughter, and handclaps.

It took me a moment to realize it was the choir of children I had come to work with. I turned off my CD and listened as their beautiful voices wafted through the window.

I lay there in awe, my sleep-deprived body desperate for rest and my tired mind trying to wrap itself around everything. Despite the exhaustion, I felt absolutely filled. I propped my head up on my hand and peered out the window that was inches from my head, but I only saw bed sheets blowing in the soft breeze.

The children continued to sing, harmonies melting into each other, backed up by energetic drumming. An occasional African chant would arise from the mix ("Ayeeayeeayee-AYE!"), and I could hear laughter and joy in each voice.

I lay back down, a world away from home and everything familiar, my soul feeling a little more settled.

14

DEVOTIONS

Later that day, I found out what the beautiful sound was. The children started and ended every day with devotions. Before the children went to bed, I had the chance to join them in the event I had heard that morning.

Standing in a big circle, five children led the group in praise and worship. Each child picked a praise song to lead, and the group sang along, clapping and dancing to the drumbeat. The children sang at the top of their lungs, cheering and laughing.

As the praise songs came to an end, each of the five children then chose a worship song to lead. Eyes closed, hands raised as high as they could go, these beautiful children once again sang with all they had in their little bodies. They lifted it all up to their God.

As I ended my first day in Uganda, I watched in amazement as my definition of worship began to redefine itself.

Devotions quickly became my favorite time of tour. The energy that these kids emanated as they worshipped was simply amazing. I was starting to learn that I wasn't a huge fan of loud, energetic worship, but in this tight-knit family, it felt right. It seemed more natural while much of the contemporary worship I participated in at home felt staged. And it was. The set was planned and songs rehearsed. I was okay with that as a worship leader because I like to plan and rehearse. But here, with my new family, each child brought whatever song they wanted to bring in that moment. I'm not good with spontaneity (I don't think well on my feet), but I was amazed at the way these children chose their songs and led them with conviction. Their ear-to-ear grins also showed me that their energy was genuine, not something staged for those watching.

I also loved the dancing, yet another thing I am usually not a fan of in worship. When I had witnessed spontaneous dancing in other worship settings, I felt like people were doing it only to show off or draw attention to themselves. Here, with these beautiful children, I loved to see them dance. It was energetic and fun. I let go of my inhibitions and danced right along with them, which usually elicited giggles from the children around me.

My favorites were the African songs. I couldn't speak a lick of Luganda, but I loved trying to keep up with the kids as they sang. I listened to the words and tried to mimic. I didn't have any idea what the songs meant, but the joy that the kids sang with was contagious.

Within a few weeks, I was singing along with all of my favorite Luganda pieces. The kids were impressed as they watched me sing.

The strange, foreign words brought intense comfort to my soul. They reminded me of the Latin sacred songs I sang in college. There was a kind of coziness in those unfamiliar words.

Mukama ye musumba wange
Asinga abasumba bona
Ela wembela nga ngwa
Anyimusa mu kwagala kwe

I had a vague idea of what the songs meant, but I was curious to the entire meaning. On our long bus rides, I asked the kids. They thought for a moment, their bright, beautiful eyes turning sideways and their mouths scrunching up in concentration. It was like an extra English lesson.

Their translations made me smile. Simple. Literal. Beautiful.

The Lord is my shepherd
Who wins all the pastors
When I fall down
He picks me up in His love

Sometimes the kids came to my side during devotions, tugging on my sleeve. I leaned down and they whispered translations into my ear.

Wamile wamil parapana Yesu...

"God is for praises."

Way zee jyu keel ah jaywanzeejah
nayfukahmaylah wanzee oomkuzinzay.

"If I remember where Jesus brought me, I
kneel down and worship."

I allowed myself to get lost in our worship time. I closed my eyes and swayed slowly back and forth. As the last song wrapped up, one child said, "Let us pray." That was the cue for the fervent, energetic prayers to begin.

On that first day in Uganda, those prayers overwhelmed me. Every child prayed out loud, at the same time, as loud and as fast as they could. I found myself unable to think, let alone pray in the midst of the cacophony.

With time, the sound of all those voices became comforting. I slipped my voice into the rhythm of theirs, offering up my prayers in the midst of all the others.

Some days, I quietly stood and listened to the prayers going up around me. I loved to hear the sweet, innocent faith of these children. They truly believed that God was hearing them and that their prayers would be answered.

"Heavenly Father, thank You for keeping us safe..."

"Lord God, please watch over my family..."

"Heavenly Father, we ask that You be with us where we go..."

As much as I enjoyed the concerts and special events and traveling to foreign cities, the best part of tour was always devotions. It was the time when this sweet extended family I had been adopted into gathered together and lifted our voices to God. And through that time, we grew closer to each other.

15

MAKINDYE REHEARSALS

I sat on a wooden table that was pushed back into a corner of the large room with concrete floors and walls. I had been in Makindye, Uganda for a week. My jet lag was a vague memory from days past, but my mind was still overwhelmed by all the sights and sounds that surrounded me. I had visited homes and schools and eaten Ugandan food. Chapati (a really thick tortilla), matoke (plantains), and rice with peanut sauce had quickly become my favorite dishes. As I had walked the dusty streets over the last several days, I heard whispers of "Mzungu," everywhere I went. It was not a derogatory term; it was simply the word for white person.

I glanced around the concrete room. Posters filled with English vocabulary lined the walls. The room was a multi-use space, where the children ate, went to school, rehearsed, and had their devotions every morning and night.

It was Saturday morning, and the choir was gathered in a circle. The dance instructor was there for their weekly lesson. He spent hours with them each week teaching them traditional dances and drumming.

He helped four of the boys tie rattles to their legs. The rattles wrapped all around their calves and looked like they were made from large walnuts. They were filled with small beads that made a loud clattering when the boys shook their legs. I would come to hate those rattles as they began to break after months of constant use. After each concert, I would crawl on hands and knees around the stage to pick up little beads that had leaked out during the dance.

While the boys were fastening the leg rattles, four girls tied on grass skirts and a fat belt that looked like an extra long neck pillow. The belts rested on their hips. I would soon learn that they created the illusion that their hips were moving more than they actually were. At least that's what the girls told me. However, I saw them move without them, and I can vouch that those hips moved just fine on their own.

Once the rattles and grass skirts were tied, the children got into their formation: a long line of children at the back, four drummers and four dancers at each side of the room.

The instructor shouted instructions, and they were off. Perched on the back table, I watched in amazement. The girls moved their arms up and down and swayed their hips like hula dancers. Jane's big smile lit up the room as she moved. My jaw almost dropped as I watched Maureen. She absolutely came alive as she danced.

The boys pranced around them, their leg rattles creating a deafening explosion of noise. They fell back on their hands into a crab walk position. They moved their legs back and forth, and those rattles rang out even louder. Peter seemed especially into it, shaking his legs as much as possible to create as much sound as he could.

My eyes drifted from the dancers to the drummers. Douglas's hands were a blur as he pounded out the rhythm on the long, skinny drum. Junior tapped away on the tiny drum with drumsticks. Frankie and Martie pounded along on the larger drums. All together, those four drums created a rhythm and music like I had never heard. The sound was full, energetic, and even harmonious. It was so different from every musical style I had ever heard before; it didn't sound like the classical arias that had filled my college days or the pop and rock music from high school, and it definitely didn't sound like CCM.

Thump, thwack, thud, rattatattatat. There were no other instruments playing, no piano or guitars, and yet there was still a melodic feel. I had always assumed the drum's only purpose was to keep the rhythm. Here, they created music all on their own. The beat buzzed through my ears and invigorated me. It made me want to jump up and dance with them, even though I could never move the way they did.

The energy in the room was incredible. I stared wide-eyed as they rehearsed all the African dances, the teacher carefully instructing them on each bit of choreography. These kids were crazy talented, and I began to grow nervous at the thought of teaching them. What could I possibly show them?

~

TWO DAYS LATER, I was standing on that concrete floor in front of those children. Abraham gave instructions to them in Luganda while I stood nervously next to him. Abraham had toured as a child in the choir and was now returning to work as a chaperone.

I wondered if I had remembered deodorant that morning as sweat dripped from my armpits. It was hot in Makindye, and the breeze floating through the open doors didn't do much to cool down the room.

The kids were familiar with me. I had spent several days

with them in devotions and eaten chapati and rice with them. I had read books to them while we sat on the front porch and they braided my hair with the breeze gently rustling the fronds of the trees just outside the concrete wall that surrounded the property. I had instructed them to line up in preparation for meals and school. But today was the first day that I was going to lead rehearsal. It was the whole reason I had volunteered for this crazy adventure. I was excited but also really nervous. I had never been much of a leader, and being in charge of 24 children and their concerts was out of my comfort zone.

Abraham finished his instructions and looked at me. "Okay Auntie. They're all yours." Then he walked to the side of the room and left me in charge. I swallowed hard.

I had made some notes and planned out what I would work on ahead of time. I had been watching them rehearse for a few days, trying to get familiar with the songs and the concert. I decided to start with "Because You Loved Me." I was familiar with the song. Celine Dion sang it, and I had been a big fan of hers in middle and high school. I had even kept a couple of her albums through my great CD purge.

"Okay," I said, my voice shaking slightly. I breathed in silently to calm my nerves.

"Let's begin with 'Because You Loved Me.' Let me hear you sing it." I walked to the boom box and hit play. The kids began to sway as the track began. I clumsily conducted them, fully aware of how awkward I looked.

They sang through the song, and I noticed a few places where the notes were flat. My brain raced through ten years of choir rehearsals and four years of music school, specifically my one brief semester of vocal pedagogy. I was supposed to know how to fix this. How *do* you fix flat notes?

I settled on breath support. That was the answer to all vocal faults.

"Um, okay..." I said. A few children cocked their heads,

waiting for my instructions. My eyes scanned the choir in front of me. I looked at Gladys in the back row. She was especially attentive. Veneranda stood on the second row, and my eyes caught her big, beautiful smile. I relaxed a bit, took in a deep breath, and then quietly exhaled it.

"Put your hands on your stomach," I commanded. I lifted my hands to my stomach in demonstration. Forty-eight hands followed my lead.

"Now, take a big breath in, and fill your stomach with the breath."

This was met with more quizzical stares. Although the kids spoke English, they were still learning a lot of words. I realized it was a little more difficult to demonstrate this action with physical gestures. I didn't want to over exaggerate the breathing since singers are supposed to take subtle but deep breaths. If I were to take a loud, audible breath, it would negate the point I was trying to make. (I also realized that asking them to fill their stomach with the breath was technically incorrect, but I wasn't ready to explain the diaphragm to them quite yet.)

I looked around helplessly, toward Uncle Abraham who was sitting nearby. He looked up and loudly repeated my instructions in Luganda. The kids nodded, suddenly understanding. I watched as the three choir rows breathed in, filling their sweet little diaphragms with air.

"Do you feel your stomach getting bigger?" I patted my stomach to emphasize my point.

My question was met with nods and choruses of "Yes, Auntie."

"Okay, keep your hands on your stomach. I want you to keep filling your stomachs as you sing. Let's try again."

I hit play on the CD player, and the song began again. The kids stood with hands on their stomachs. I watched as a few shoulders rose with their breath.

"Keep those shoulders still! I only want to see stomachs moving!"

That instruction was met with a few quizzical stares, so I walked between the first and second row and put my hands on a few shoulders.

"Don't move these," I put my hands on Ruthy's shoulders. "Fill these." I patted Brenda's tummy and heard a few giggles around me.

As they sang through the song, I heard the pitches improve. *I can do this!* I thought to myself.

Then, they began singing the second verse, and I heard the pitches begin to flatten again.

"Keep breathing!" I shouted, trying to remain energetic and optimistic.

The pitches didn't get any better.

I returned to the front of the choir, once again racking my brain for a way to fix it. I spent the rest of the rehearsal time flustered, trying to come up with creative ways to fix the vocal issues I heard. The kids were patient and stood quietly as I fumbled through instructions. They tried each and every weird idea I had. We sang the phrases on "doo" in the hopes that they would focus on pitch instead of words. We practiced holding our breath to work on breath control. I even asked them to simply think higher. At the end of rehearsal, the pitch was still flat.

As the kids lined up for dinner, I felt frustrated that my ideas hadn't worked. I wondered how effective I was going to be on this tour. I closed my eyes and sent up a silent prayer for help.

~

A WEEK AND A HALF LATER, the choir, other chaperones, and I were recovering from jet lag in Washington state. Tour had officially begun, and the choir was preparing for its first concert. The kids were excited; I was nervous. I was still figuring out my duties as music supervisor, and I wasn't sure what to expect. A music supervisor from a previous choir was with us for that first concert, helping us get the kids ready for the stage. I was glad she was there, especially when she offered to warm the kids up vocally. It gave me a chance to relax a bit and see how the concert schedule would flow.

We stuffed into a Sunday school room in the back of the church. Cartoon Bible characters lined the walls along with Scripture verses. Tiny tables and chairs were stacked on top of each other and pushed against the walls so that the kids would have enough room for their three choir rows.

We did devotions, warm ups, and a pre-concert pep talk in that tiny room. Craig, one of my fellow chaperones, was in the sanctuary, and he gave us the signal to line up through our radios. I stood watching as the kids moved from their concert rows into two lines. We silently walked down the church hallway toward the sanctuary, the kids with one finger over their lips (they needed that extra reminder to walk quietly).

The kids got into position outside the sanctuary doors and waited for their cue. The voice of Ray Barnett (Daddy Ray to the kids) echoed through the sanctuary. He was the founder of the choir, and his recorded audio would introduce the 25th African Children's Choir for the duration of our tour. As soon as the audio ended, the kids whizzed by me, squealing their African chants and clapping their way to the stage.

I watched in amazement as they danced all over the stage. I had seen this concert many times in the concrete room in Makindye, but it was a whole different experience on stage with spotlights brightening up their beautiful smiles. My throat tightened as I watched the audience cheer and rise to its feet. The more the audience cheered, the bigger the kids smiled. I swelled with pride as I watched Moriah and Alex perform their solos. They started out tentatively, but their confidence grew as the song progressed.

When the kids finished their final song, the audience rose to their feet in roaring applause. I grew excited at the prospect of the tour that lay ahead. These were *my* kids, and I couldn't wait to work with them.

PART VI

CADENCE

16

TOUR LIFE

Two months later, I stood back in front of three choir rows. I had led dozens of rehearsals since that first one in Makindye. They still made me a bit anxious, but I was beginning to enjoy them more.

They watched me, waiting for instructions. It was time for warm-ups. I thought back to all the weird scales and vowels I was made to sing through my years of choir rehearsals. I decided to begin with something simple.

"Okay, my turn, your turn." I pointed to myself and then to them as I said these words to emphasize my point. "My turn." I moved the pointing finger toward me and begin to sing.

"Meeeee-Ahhhh..." I glided up a five-note scale and back down.

"Your turn." My finger turned toward them.

"Meeee-Ahhhh!" The kids loudly imitated my sound. I loved their eagerness and the joy in their singing, which was evident in something as simple as a five-note scale warm-up.

"Not bad. Can you sing a little lighter? You sound like you're shouting at me. MEEEEEEE-AHHHHHHH!" I imitated their sound, loud and overly dramatic to prove my point. A couple kids jumped and giggled.

"Sing it softer." I repeated the five-note phrase, singing it softer and lighter. I pointed to them again, indicating their turn. They sang the phrase back to me, this time softer.

"Much better! That sounds much nicer." I pointed to myself again and sang another five-note scale, half a note up.

"Meeee-Ahhhh..."

They repeated back to me. Their volume was better, but I also wanted them to create more space in their mouth for a better vowel sound and to allow for better breath flow.

I raised my hands to my cheeks. "Put your hands on your face," I instructed. The children's hands rose up to their beautiful, brown cheeks.

"Good. Now drop your jaw down." I demonstrated again. Jaws popped open, some wide and others only partway.

"Act like you're surprised," I offered a silly surprised face for an example. Again, giggles tittered from the choir rows in front of me. Surprised faces popped up from child to child, and they laughed some more as they modeled their faces for each other.

I couldn't help but laugh myself. "Very nice. Now, keep your hands on your face and that jaw down. And sing... Meeee-Ahhh..."

Twenty-four children echoed my sound. It was richer and more uniform.

"Can you hear the difference?" Heads nodded. "You have more space in your mouth, and it makes the sound nicer. So when you sing, you should always sound like this," (I sang with an open mouth) "rather than this." (I narrowed my jaw and sang thin and ugly.)

The kids nodded.

"Let me hear you again."

We sang the exercise several more times, going up half a step in between each one. Then I moved on to another warm up. I thought back to one of my favorites from high school choir.

Zing-a-mama-zing-a-mama-zing-a-
mama-zing-a-mama-zing-zing-zing!

I would use this warm up so much that Auntie Emily affectionately nicknamed me Zingamama.

The kids giggled at the ridiculous words but sang them back to me beautifully. Again, we sang the exercise over and over, moving either up or down a half step each time.

"Give me good diction!" I shouted above their vocals. "I want to hear you e-nun-ci-ate!" I saw heads nod. Their English had already come a long way in just a couple months. I was starting to throw more big words their way, and they were retaining them.

"Okay," I said. "Let's move onto a song. Let's work on 'You Are the Shepherd.'" I walked to the boom box and hit track five. I returned to the front of the choir and raised my hands to a conductor's position, indicating that the children should be ready. They stood up straight and looked toward me, ready to begin. The instrumental track played the introduction, and the kids began to sing.

"Yoooou ahhhh-re the Shepherd . . . " They swayed back and forth as the slow instrumental track played. I shouted instructions over the music.

"Remember to smile!" I gave them a big goofy grin as an example. "Eyes up here, Martin!" Martin sheepishly smiled and returned his eyes to me.

The song finished, and I pushed the stop button on the CD player. "Not bad." I thought for a minute, deciding what to work on first.

"You are still singing so heavy, so loud." My mind raced, trying to figure out how to get my point across.

"How many of you have a baby brother or sister?" Several hands went up. "Do you know what a lullaby is?" Heads shook.

"A lullaby is a song to help put a baby to sleep." I raised my arms and cradled them to my chest, rocking an imaginary baby. "When you sing to a baby, you want to sing quietly and softly, to soothe them. This is how you are singing to your baby: YOOOOU AHHHH-RE THE SHEPHERD!!" I sang loudly and made several jump again. More giggles. Some children put their hands to their mouth in an effort to stifle their laughter.

"You are scaring your children! The babies are not sleeping. They are now crying."

More giggles.

"I want you to pretend that you are holding a baby. Hold up your arms." The kids raised their arms and held their pretend babies. "I'm going to start the music again." I lowered my voice to a near whisper so that kids had to lean forward to hear. "Sing this song to your baby."

The kids cradled and swooned as they sang over their pretend babies. Their eyes brightened as they imagined the sweet little infants in their charge. Stella snuggled her baby especially tight to her chest.

"You aaaahre the Shepherd," a beautiful sound floated through the sanctuary and bounced off the walls.

They sang quieter. It worked.

"Yes!" I said. "Did you hear the difference?" The kids nodded excitedly. "I want you to sing it that way every time."

Rehearsal was over before I realized my nerves had completely subsided.

~

LATER THAT DAY, I was on an improvised soccer field complete with sweatshirts for makeshift goal posts. Frank and Lawrence ran around in their undershirts, gladly sacrificing their outerwear for the love of the game.

I was getting my butt kicked by nine year olds. I couldn't seem to keep up with the energy of the boys and girls around me. They laughed as I tried and usually failed to get the ball from them. Zig-zagging around me with incredible accuracy, they taunted and tempted me to chase after them. If I ever did succeed in getting the ball, I couldn't seem to hold onto it.

After 30 minutes of intense running, I collapsed onto the grass, gasping for breath while 15 children latched onto me with cries of, "Eeee! Auntie!" Their laughter made me smile as they regaled me with stories of how I couldn't keep the ball . . . as if I needed a reminder.

As playtime wound to a close, we marched back into the church that was our home base for the day. The children returned to their classrooms. It was time for me to put on my next hat: English teacher. Playtime was over; it was time for English vocabulary.

The children opened their books, and we began a discussion on parts of the body. My goal for this lesson was to have them recognize the words for body parts and hopefully spell a few correctly.

I drew a crude stick figure on the board. Snickers came from behind me. My artwork left something to be desired. I started at the head and labeled parts of the body so the kids could identify the words. Ear, eye, throat. I got down to the stomach and heard protests behind me.

"Eee, Auntie, that is stow-mach!" Dorothy pronounced the word phonetically, emphasizing the "ch" sound. The kids laughed. They thought I was playing a trick on them.

I assured them that this was how stomach was spelled and not "stomak" as many of them kept insisting. We continued with the lesson, and I urged them to draw their own diagram in their book, writing down the correct spelling of each body part.

They huddled over their composition books, pencils clutched tightly in their hands. I walked around the room, looking over shoulders and checking their spelling.

I peered at one drawing and commented, "Eh, a big cabena." The whole room erupted into laughter. Felista threw her head back and laughed a little louder than everyone else. I had learned a few Luganda words, and the word for "butt" was always a crowd pleaser.

For the remainder of the hour, I drilled them on the spelling words, and they completed exercises in their books. As the lesson wound to a close, the children packed up their books, and we prepared to go home with our host families.

This crazy life was becoming my new normal, and I loved every bit of it.

~

I WAS INCREDIBLY thankful for the kindness of the host families we stayed with each evening, but making small talks with strangers did exhaust me. At the conclusion of each concert, I would slap on my "host family smile" and prepare to meet the next set of strangers that would give me a place to sleep.

I met some amazing people, like the Canadian widow who gave up her bed for me, made me soak in a hot bath for 20 minutes, and then served me chocolate cake. Or the host auntie in Madison, Wisconsin, who made me a cozy bed on the softest sofa I have ever slept on. In the morning, she quietly slipped into my room and set a cup of tea next to me while I had my quiet time. In the evening, she invited her musician friends over, and I listened with rapt attention as they played folk songs on guitars and unique drums I had never seen.

I also had some incredibly bizarre experiences like when I stayed in a home in Alaska that wasn't fully built. It had no drywall or indoor plumbing, and I had to climb a ladder to get to my third floor bedroom, while lugging my suitcase. Or when I stayed in a home that could have been on an episode of *Hoarders*. That home also featured the pet I affectionately dubbed "Satan Kitty." I love cats, but the devil himself most likely possessed this fuzzy little one. He was not pleased about me being in his home. He made that clear with his blood-curdling scream at two in the morning when I tried to use the bathroom.

Six months into tour, we finished another concert in Canada and met yet another host family. I mustered up all the professionalism and politeness that I could despite the fact that my body and soul felt completely worn out. The novelty of traveling had slowly begun to wear off and drag me down. I was also tired of the small talk.

The host uncle seemed kind. He gave big hugs to the children and a polite handshake to me. We lugged our heavy bags to the host family car. He helped us pile the luggage in the trunk, and the girls then piled into the back seat. I took my usual spot in the front next to the host uncle.

The car ride to the house was a typical one filled with questions about how I got involved with the choir, how the children were selected, and what happened when they returned home. I rattled off my answers without even thinking. These questions came on a nightly basis, and I was used to answering them over and over.

We arrived at the house and met the rest of the host family. They warmly welcomed us, and the girls began their nightly ritual of showers, snacks, and bedtime.

The host uncle showed me to my room, which was in the basement. My heart sank as we descended the stairs. The lighting became darker as we walked down. We entered a room with one bare bulb hanging from exposed wires. My bedroom for the evening was a small square room with one twin bed and a small nightstand. Instead of brightly painted walls, there was bare drywall. There was no fuzzy carpet under my toes, just a bare, cold subfloor. I forced a smile as I thanked him.

He closed the door and said goodnight. I sat on the bed and felt the springs under me. I was so tired that I probably wouldn't even feel them, but I still longed for a softer bed. I tried to focus on the fact that I had a roof over my head and a place to sleep.

But some nights, after another long, hard day of tour, it was so difficult to focus on those positive things. All I wanted was a comfy bed in a cozy little room with soft lighting and beautiful landscape photography hanging from the walls. Sometimes the little things like bare walls and a lone, swinging light bulb weighed my heart down. I sighed and unzipped my suitcase, pulling out my PJs and settling into my home for the evening.

I got a good enough night's sleep in my basement bedroom and awoke refreshed. I went upstairs to wake the girls. It was Saturday, and we had the morning off. The host families had planned a picnic for the entire choir. The weather was beautiful, and the thought of spending a morning basking in the sunshine while the kids ran some energy off on the playground sounded wonderful.

When we arrived at the park, the kids rushed out of the car to play soccer and dodgeball with their friends. I took the rare chance to relax, exhaling audibly as I sat on a picnic bench. My host uncle sat next to me. I was a bit annoyed as I had hoped for a few moments of quiet without having to answer more questions. I gritted my teeth and reminded myself that this man had graciously let me stay in his home and eat his food.

We began to chat. He mentioned that he had a music business and had done some recording. My eyes lit up as I heard this.

"I've done a bit of recording myself. And dabbled in songwriting too."

He smiled. "What kind of songs do you write?"

"Christian music. I mainly write lyrics but also sometimes melodies. I've started to learn guitar, but I'm not very good. I have a friend that plays guitar really well, and he and I have co-written some songs."

Then my heart fell as I realized I couldn't remember the last time I had tried to write a song.

"Unfortunately, I haven't written much lately. The chaotic nature of tour doesn't always lend well to creativeness and songwriting."

He gave me a small smile. "I can imagine it would be hard to find time to write while on an adventure like this."

I nodded and looked toward the soccer field where the playful squeals of my children echoed across the park.

"Yeah, but I sure wouldn't trade it for anything."

We sat in silence for a few moments. Then he spoke again.

"Can I pray for you?"

And there in the warmth of the Canadian sunshine, he prayed for me. He prayed for the music that I would make and the future songs I would write. As he prayed, I began to feel guilty for my ungratefulness toward my basement bedroom. I was reminded yet again of the graciousness of every person we met on tour.

17

SECULAR MUSICIANS

Each day on tour was an adventure: new cities, new sights, new host families, new places to explore. It was exciting, and about a year into tour, we found ourselves presented with some huge opportunities. The choir was asked to perform with Wyclef Jean on *The Tonight Show* with Jay Leno and *Ellen*. Wyclef had recorded a song for the *Hotel Rwanda* soundtrack that featured a choir of African children. He wanted a live choir to perform the song with him for his television appearances. We were in Los Angeles at the time, so it worked out perfectly.

As we waited backstage at NBC's television studio, I tittered around nervously, hoping that we had prepared the children enough. Famous people walked in and out of the room all afternoon, cooing over the kids. At least I assumed they were famous. I didn't recognize them, but they were dressed in trendy clothing and had impeccable makeup. Probably some TV star from a show I hadn't seen. I had fallen out of touch with popular culture, partly from my insistence on boxing myself into CCM culture but also because I was so busy on tour that I just couldn't keep up.

I walked to a mirror and fluffed my hair and applied some lip-gloss in the hopes that I would look a little less frumpy. Emily moved in next to me and did the same. We looked at each other and laughed nervously. We were wearing our usual uniform: black pants and embroidered button up shirts with the African Children's Choir logo. It looked professional, but we felt shabby next to the celebrities that flowed in and out all day.

We moved to the studio for rehearsal, and I walked around in awe looking at the huge cameras and lights. I was so out of my element.

Wyclef Jean strolled out with his electric guitar in hand. I didn't even know who Wyclef was until someone told me he had sung with the Fugees. I remembered them vaguely from high school, mainly from their cover of "Killing Me Softly." He seemed nice enough, but he was a secular musician, so I was wary. I looked at the performance as an opportunity for my kids to share the love of Christ with him and with the world that would watch.

The song featured a chorus in a Rwandan language. The chorus was the choir's part, and Uncle Abraham had taught it to them in the last week. The rest of the song spoke of a longing for peace in Africa, specifically against the Rwandan genocide. The kids would sing the verses over and over for weeks to come.

The choir ran through the song with Wyclef and his band. I was so proud as they sang powerfully, all while dancing to the beat. I know the cameras and lights overwhelmed them, but they didn't let it deter their focus.

After rehearsal, we returned to our green room for another couple hours of waiting. We wanted to keep as much of a routine for the kids as possible, so we decided to have school in the TV studio. But we knew the day would be distracting, so we kept it low key and let the kids write letters to their families at home. They eagerly dove into the task, concentrating heavily on their papers in front of them.

Famous people continued to pour in and out of the room, eager for a chance to dote on the African children. I watched as the kids were completely unfazed by the celebrities around them. They looked up and politely greeted the adults that came in the room but then immediately returned their attention to their letters. Ruth was especially focused on the crayons scattered on the table, looking for the perfect shade of blue to finish her picture.

When it came time for the performance, the kids along with Uncle Abraham (he would conduct them from behind the cameras) were taken out to the stage. The rest of the chaperones were ushered to the back of the studio behind the audience to watch. I stood in the darkness of that back corner and watched excitedly as Jay Leno introduced Wyclef Jean and the African Children's Choir.

The curtains rose, and the bright lights revealed Wyclef and his band. I laughed as I realized that Wyclef was wearing an African Children's Choir t-shirt. And standing directly behind him were my kids, my beautiful, talented children. Their smiles lit up the room more than the stage lights.

My eyes drifted from Joseph to Christine to Joan to Gorrett. They sang beautifully, danced with incredible energy, and radiated hope. I was so proud I could burst. I wanted to shake the shoulders of the people I stood behind and tell them, "Those are *my* kids!"

When the song finished, the audience burst into applause. I clapped louder than everyone.

~

A LITTLE OVER a year into my time on tour, I was asked to join another choir as their music supervisor. I was sad to leave my kids, but I felt that the move was right. Holly, another chaperone, was also asked to join the new choir. Having a friend come along made the decision a little easier.

The last few weeks with this choir were filled with busy, hectic events. It kept my mind off the inevitable goodbye that was approaching, but part of me desperately wanted quiet to process.

One of the events was a special program for the organization ONEXONE, which was started by several Hollywood actors in an effort to alleviate poverty. The event was part of the 2005 Toronto International Film Festival. We gathered at the Toronto Distillery District to begin rehearsals.

We sang with Chantal Kreviazuk, a Canadian singer-songwriter. For rehearsal, she sat at a large grand piano with the kids gathered around. She began to play her song "What If It All Means Something." I watched her with envy as her hands effortlessly moved between the keys. I could play a little but had never managed to move beyond average, much like my guitar skills.

She began to sing the verses, and I listened to her powerful voice reverberate throughout the small room we were cramped into. She motioned toward the kids to begin singing on the chorus.

We had received the song ahead of time, so the kids already knew their part. They sang the melody with confidence, and I beamed with pride as she praised them for their vocal quality and how well they had learned the song.

A tiny part of me was surprised that she was so kind and gracious. It was like I expected secular musicians to be self-absorbed because they weren't singing directly about the love of Christ.

After she finished running the song a second time, she said, "I have another song I want to teach you. I think you can learn it pretty quick. First, I want to tell you about a man named Bob Marley."

She then proceeded to tell the story of Marley, how he had fought back against war and hate with the power of love and music. I had never listened to Bob Marley. He was a pot-smoking hippie, and his music was evil, at least that's what I always assumed. The Christian subculture I had surrounded myself with had taught me that anyone doing drugs should not be listened to.

Chantal began to sing the chorus to Bob Marley's song "Redemption Songs." I bristled at the fact that she was teaching it to my children. I listened to the cryptic lyrics, and for a moment, I was that insecure teenager, surrounded by music I didn't understand.

But there was something in the way she sang the melody that drew me in. It was smooth, easy, and pure. Her voice glided through the air, the notes floating above us like a bird caught on gusts of air. The sound brought me peace and calm. She was passionate, and I could tell she felt a deep connection to the words she sang. The more I listened, the more I realized they were poetry. I didn't fully understand the words, but I realized that was okay. They still intrigued me. And if this man had fought against hate and war with music, like Chantal said, how could he be bad?

I relaxed further as I appreciated that I was in a rehearsal where I didn't have to be in charge. I stood in the back and listened as she sang the chorus to the kids.

The kids grabbed onto the melody quickly and listened with rapt attention as Chantal sang the verses. As she began each chorus, she motioned with her head for the kids to join in. They did, singing at the top of their lungs. The adults joined in too. Those songs of freedom were begging to be sung.

In the end, I was thankful to Chantal for teaching that song to my kids and to me. I stood there transfixed by the beautiful melody and intoxicating lyrics of a pot-smoking hippie.

HOURS LATER, we rehearsed with the band Our Lady Peace. The lead singer was Chantal's husband. I remembered Our Lady Peace from high school. A few of their songs were in rotation on the 90s alternative station that I would hear as I hitched rides to school. I never had any of their albums, but if I had, they would have been ousted in the Great CD Purge of '98.

As we rehearsed, I was impressed with their sound. It was fun with rollicking guitar solos and enthusiastic vocals. The band members were amusing, cracking jokes with the kids. They didn't strike me as the 90s alternative musician that I had always pictured. I had envisioned a depressed, overly-tattooed, brooding group of musicians to go along with the self-deprecating music. Our Lady Peace seemed happy and well-adjusted. I watched as they threw their heads back in laughter and made funny faces for my kids.

The band began playing their song "Innocent," which would be the finale of the ONEXONE event. My kids danced to the beat and strummed air guitars. Several watched the drummer pounding on the snare drum and cymbals and began to imitate him with imaginary drumsticks in hand.

As the chorus began, Raine Maida, the lead singer, pointed to the kids and said, "Here's your part!"

The kids picked up the melody quickly and joined in, singing loudly through grinning faces. They were singing a secular song and doing it with such joy. By the second chorus, the kids had gained even more confidence on the melody. They sang it loud and with gusto.

The band started the song again to make sure the kids were comfortable. Not only had they learned their part in the chorus, they started to sing along with the pre-chorus, belting out the high note at the beginning of each phrase. Raine laughed and shouted into the microphone, "I like it!"

Twenty minutes later, rehearsal wrapped up. I stood with two fingers raised in the air to get the kids lined up for a bathroom break. Before getting in line, they ran over to hug each member of the band. The band's faces lit up as they each received 24 furious hugs. They hugged back tightly, and one wiped a tear from his cheek.

AFTER A WHIRLWIND few days of rehearsal, the day of the event arrived. A large tent in the middle of a parking lot was transformed into an elegant reception space. Trendy white curtains draped the sides of the stage. A huge banner over the stage proclaimed ONEXONE. Colorful lights were artistically placed, accenting the banner and the musicians who would later don the stage. Tables were set with white linens, fine china, and a large floral centerpiece. Trendy clear chairs surrounded the tables. I knew that I would not be sitting at those tables and wondered how much the event cost.

Kate Hudson was the host for the evening, and I snapped a few pictures of her back from a distance as she hugged my kids. The rest of the evening was a total blur. I was exhausted, overwhelmed, and moody. Celebrities were walking by me, and I didn't care. I was too tired to be star struck. I wanted to be snuggled up in a hotel bed, reading a bedtime story to my kids. Taking a deep breath, I focused on my job of getting the kids warmed up and on stage at the right time.

During one of their performances, I stood to the side of the stage and watched. Memories from the last 15 months flooded my mind, and I blinked back tears. I wiped the lone tear that managed to escape. There was a large man standing to my right, dressed in black and with an earpiece. Bouncer, I supposed.

He leaned over and smiled at me. Then in a husky voice he asked, "You okay?"

I was thankful for the simple fact that I was noticed in this vast, crazy crowd. For days, celebrities had hugged my kids and posed for photo ops while they completely ignored me. They were perfectly made up with stylish clothes and accessories. I felt invisible in my tattered button up shirt with the embroidered Auntie Jamie label.

Part of me wanted to open up and leave a puddle of tears at this man's feet. I wanted to tell him how I was going to have to leave these kids in just a few short days, about how important they were to me, how I didn't know how to get through the goodbye. I decided he probably didn't have time for that right then. I didn't have time either because in less than a minute my kids would be bounding off the stage and I had to take them to yet another bathroom break.

"Yeah, just tired," I responded with a weak smile.

He nodded in acknowledgement, and our conversation ended there. The kids raced off the stage. Duty called again.

Hours later, we finished the concert. My head was ringing, and the tears were getting harder to fight back. On the bus ride back to our home for the evening, the kids continued to sing. I heard medleys of songs bouncing off the bus walls.

We slept in sleeping bags on a high school gym floor. I tried not to be resentful as I thought about the famous people that hugged all over my kids just hours before and were now peacefully sleeping in some ritzy hotel. I pulled the sleeping bag higher over my shoulders and sniffled back a few tears.

~

Several days later, I began what was to be one of the hardest days of my life. With a huge lump in my throat and a giant knot in my stomach, I hugged my kids for the last time. I tried to be strong and choked back tears as I left them with some tender, parting words. As I walked away, the sobs wracked my body. A kind stranger pulled me into her arms and gave me a tight hug. She was a member of a host family and said to me, "You poor dear. I'm sad to leave them after two days with them. I can't imagine how you must feel."

Someone else ushered Holly and me into a minivan and gently pressed an entire box of tissues into my hands. The ride to the airport was a blur as I blinked away the constant flow of tears.

I took a deep breath and readied myself to meet a new choir of kids to love on.

18

CCM MUSICIANS

Two months into my second choir's tour, we received big news. We were going to record with the Gaithers. Benji Gaither, son of Bill & Gloria Gaither, wanted us to record backing vocals for a song off their upcoming album.

The Gaithers had been hugely influential in Christian and gospel music over the last several decades. Though not a huge Gaither fan, I knew the impact they had had on my precious CCM genre. I was excited for the opportunity and also curious about being inside a professional recording studio.

With only a few days to learn a song and teach three-part harmony, I dove in. Luckily, I was used to working under pressure, having done it several times with my last choir. We had learned a lot of music in a short time, so I knew it could be done.

While the kids were out at playtime, I sat at a piano in a quiet sanctuary somewhere in Illinois. After being on tour for over a year, I had stopped keeping track of our travel itinerary. I barely kept up with where we going, and sometimes couldn't even remember where we were.

With my headphones in, I listened to the song over and

over, picking out harmony parts. I found myself thankful for the ear training that I so despised while taking it in college two years prior. I plunked away on the keyboard, picking out the melody line and penciling it on blank sheet music. Once I figured out the melody, I built harmony parts around it. I've always been a visual learner, so writing out all the parts was the easiest way for me to create harmonies and to remember them well enough to teach them to the kids.

As I hit the play button for about the 50th time, I began to grow irritated at the song. It seemed especially cheesy, even by CCM standards. The lyrics in particular bugged me.

If coal can turn to diamonds
And sand can turn to pearls
If a worm can turn into a butterfly
Then love can turn the world
Oh, love can turn the world

I was really annoyed at the worm line, especially after sharing the song with my fellow chaperones. Sharye said it best: "Worms don't turn into butterflies!" I understood that caterpillar was hard to fit into the rhythm of the vocal line, but the blatant error in the text still annoyed me. I was also really tired of the song in general. I knew that the melody line would follow me for days. That dumb worm line had become an earworm.

The next day, I began to teach the harmonies to the kids. They patiently listened and tried to recreate it. Some grew fidgety as we worked on it all morning and into the afternoon. By the end of the day, they had a satisfactory three-part harmony. Not perfect, but pretty darn good for kids who had only been on tour for two months.

We rehearsed the song again the following day. After

rehearsal, the kids walked around singing it to each other. They sang it all day long.

> *If a worm can turn into a butterfly*
> *Then love can turn the world*

I rubbed my temples. I was really tired of the song.

At least they learned it, I told myself.

~

WHEN WE ARRIVED at Gaither studios the next day, the woman at the front desk asked if the kids had heard the song. I stared at her, trying to mask my disbelief. They did tell us they wanted three-part harmony, right?

"Uh, yes, they've heard the song. We have three part harmonies worked out."

She smiled as she glanced up from her computer. I wanted to add that we had been listening to the song on repeat for the last two days straight and if I heard it one more time I was going to snap. I chose to keep that nugget to myself.

Once inside, Benji Gaither greeted us. I shook his hand and motioned toward the kids to introduce them. Then he got a proper African Children's Choir greeting: 25 very tight and energetic hugs.

"I can't wait to hear you guys!" he said. Turning to me, he added, "There are a few extra things I'd like to add. Can the kids sing the last line in their language?"

"Uh, yeah, we can do that," was what came out of my mouth. In my mind, I thought, *A little advance notice would have been nice.* The difficult part was that this choir came from two different countries and spoke two different languages. There was no singing it in "their" language. I turned to Lydia and Jerusha, the two African chaperones on our team. Lydia was from Uganda and Jerusha from Kenya. They had both traveled with the choir as kids and were now working as chaperones. We had a quick meeting and agreed that they would each translate the chorus and the language that best fit into the rhythm would win.

They retreated to a corner and began the task of translating the text into Luganda and Swahili. Within about ten minutes, they had translations completed. Luganda won.

While they worked on the translations, Benji sat at a piano so that the kids could run through the song with him. He played through some chords and scales, and then said out loud to himself, "Hmmm, what key was it in?"

"Um... D," I informed him. Having listened to the song about 100 times over the last three days I was well aware of the key.

He played a D chord and then the intro to the song. "Ah! There it is!" I was surprised at how unprepared he seemed and the minimal amount of communication we had received prior to the day of recording. At the same time, I was proud of how prepared and professional we were.

He played through the song, guiding the kids on their part. They busted out their three-part harmony, and he seemed to like what he heard. I breathed a silent sigh of relief. Lydia then joined us to teach them the Luganda line. Even the Kenyan kids picked up on it quickly.

Then the fun part began. They set the kids up in front of the microphones and gave each one their own headset. Their grins swallowed up what part of their face the headphones didn't. They began to chatter to each other and then exclaimed, "Eh eh?!" in surprise when they heard their own voices in their headphones. Gift looked around in wonder at all the recording equipment around us.

They handed me and Lydia headsets too. I would conduct, and Lydia would help with the Luganda line. My hands were shaking as I slipped my headphones over my ears. The realization that we were about to record on a major CCM musician's album began to sink in; also that the writer of the song was standing behind me in the booth, watching my every move. No pressure. Craig came out and handed me a bottle of water. He grinned, gave me a thumb's up, and returned to the booth. I took a swig of water and a deep breath.

The track began, and I looked at the kids and gave them a big smile of encouragement. I had only been with them for a couple months but already their sweet smiles and unique personalities had melted my heart. I thought back to our first few days together in sleeping bags on a church sanctuary floor. We had spent several days getting to know each other as the kids recovered from jet lag and the chaperones passed out socks and toothpaste to fill their new duffel bags.

The kids had quickly learned about microphones and stage lights. They only had a handful of performances under their belt, but their musicality still amazed me. And now, here they were, in a professional recording studio about to record on a well-known Christian artist's album. As I stood before them, grinning like an idiot, they grinned right back. I stifled laughter as Timothy's headphones fell off because his tiny little head wasn't big enough to hold them. Emmanuel stood straight and tall, smiling and completely focused on me. He was ready to go.

All of a sudden, I didn't care what any professional musician thought of these kids and their performance. As far as I was concerned, *they* were the professional musicians, learning a new song in two days flat and then rolling with last minute changes. And they did it without a bit of complaining. I was so proud of them.

The kids sang through their first take. There was a brief moment of silence, and then I heard compliments in my headphones from Benji and several of the men in the booth. They liked what they heard. They started the track again, and we sang through another take. Benji then asked for an extra high part, singing it into a mic so the kids could hear it through their headphones. Yet again, the kids learned it quickly and performed it without a word of complaint. Then Lydia conducted them for the Luganda part. Before I knew it, we were all done.

We snapped some pictures (the kids wanted their headphones on), and then we all piled into the recording booth to hear the finished product. I loved seeing the professional booth with all the knobs and switches. I saw some of the kids' eyes grow wide at all the buttons. I shot some of them a look that stated, "DO NOT TOUCH." They made eye contact with me and clearly got the message.

As they played the recording back, the kids' faces lit up as their own voices played through the speakers. "Eh, eh! That is not us!" they exclaimed.

We thanked Benji and all the staff for a fun afternoon. They thanked us for our hard work, and each of the staff members relished their goodbye hugs from the kids.

I walked out the door and looked at all the pictures on the wall of famous Christian musicians. My mind began to daydream, and I visualized my picture on that wall too. Apparently my dream of being a CCM artist was still alive.

~

AFTER RECORDING WITH THE GAITHERS, I prayed and asked God for a chance to record with some more Christian artists. I specifically prayed for an opportunity with Steven Curtis Chapman.

Weeks later, Jessica, our tour leader, approached me with a mischievous smile.

"Hey, Auntie!" We always referred to each other as Auntie or Uncle, even when the kids weren't around. "Guess what?"

I looked up from the concert notes I was studying. I noticed her playful look, and my eyebrows rose. "What?"

"I just got an interesting phone call. We have another request for recording."

"Okay," I replied, jotting down a note in the margins of my notebook. "Who's it with?"

She grinned. "Guess."

My mind raced, and I thought back to the prayer I had prayed. I was almost afraid to say it. As if saying it might make it untrue.

I looked up. Jessica was still grinning. "Steven?" I asked hesitantly.

Jessica responded with an even bigger grin.

"You so better not be teasing me!" I practically shouted.

She wasn't. Steven Curtis Chapman wanted us to record with him... at his home. I jumped up and down in excitement and grabbed Jessica by the arms. Squealing, I pulled her into a hug. She laughed and hugged me back.

Shortly after accepting the invitation, we received a CD from Steven himself with a special greeting ("Hi African Children's Choir! We're so excited to have you come!") and all the parts laid out for us. It made my job so much easier, and I was grateful that I didn't have to pick out three-part harmony again. There were specific instructions on what the kids would sing. I didn't have to do much work at all. The CD that Steven had prepared walked through each song with him clearly singing each part. In rehearsal, I just hit play and let the kids listen and sing along.

The morning of the recording, I spent time fidgeting with my hair and make-up, trying to look pretty and professional and also like I didn't try too hard. I didn't have a choice with my clothes. I pulled out my usual uniform, my faded green Auntie Jamie polo shirt and a pair of jeans, thinking about how many washing machines they had seen over the last year.

We did devotions on the bus, and I tried to focus and sing along, but I was too anxious and fidgety. I knew that Steven was just another guy, but I was still beyond excited to meet him. I thought about *The Great Adventure* CD that I received so many years ago, the album that challenged me to dig deeper into my faith. My mind also drifted back to the concert in Pensacola, where I made the decision to pursue music. Sure, he was just another guy, but he was a guy that had impacted my life in many ways.

We pulled into a long driveway with a beautiful house, fountain, large field with soccer goals (the kids were already shouting with joy over that), and a large barn. Auntie Jessica shouted from the front of the bus, "Look, Auntie Jamie! It's Uncle Steven's house!" They all knew how excited I was.

"I'm looking!" I shouted from the back of the bus.

The bus pulled to a stop by the barn, and I saw Steven step outside. My heart began to pound, and I got off the bus with several of the other chaperones. Steven approached with a warm smile.

"Thank you so much for being here!" he said in his warm Southern drawl.

I hoped that he couldn't hear my heart pounding out of my chest. I reminded myself yet again that he was a normal guy. Standing next to him, with no spotlights and in normal street clothes, it was a little easier to see that.

We entered the barn, which was actually a recording studio. I set to work, lining the kids up to do a few vocal warm ups. I did a few quick scales, then some harmony parts. "Hallelujah... Glory... Amen!" echoed off the barn walls in three-part harmony.

I was suddenly aware of someone standing to my right. Steven was there, guitar in hand.

"You sound great!" he said.

You ain't heard nothing yet, I thought to myself. Once again, I found myself insanely proud of my little group of professional musicians.

Turning to me, Steven asked, "Do you want to run through the songs on guitar?"

"Yeah, that'd be good," I replied. I was starting to breathe a little easier, and my heart wasn't pounding quite as hard. I still wanted to pinch myself.

Steven started playing and sang along with the kids while I conducted. I tried to focus on my kids in front of me, reminding them to smile and holding my hands to my jaws, a cue to open their mouths wider. I watched their eyes bounce from me to Steven. They were clearly intrigued by the guitar.

After warming up, we moved to the set where the kids would be recorded. Our recording was going to be used on Steven's upcoming tour. Not only would there be an audio recording, but there would be a video recording as well. There were cameras on stands and lights all over. My mind swirled as I got the kids set up.

We began the first song, "The Music of Christmas." It was a song I knew well from Steven's first Christmas album. It had become one of my favorite Christmas albums ever since receiving it in 1995. My mom had bought it as a Christmas gift but decided to give it to me early so I could listen to it through the Christmas season. I listened to that album over and over that December and many Decembers after that.

The kids began singing weakly. I could tell that the cameras were distracting them. I reminded them of some things that we worked on: rounding their vowels, speaking the words clearly, taking deep breaths, and singing with more energy. I also reminded them to keep their eyes on me, telling them that when they wandered the whites of their eyes gave them away. I gave them a comically overacted imitation with my eyes bouncing all over, and the kids laughed at how silly I looked.

"You will look that silly too, yes?" I asked.

The chorus of voices responded, "Yes, Auntie."

Steven joined the kids to get video footage in the midst of them. I was now conducting Steven Curtis Chapman.

"Are you going to sway with the kids?" I asked.

"I'm going to try!" he said with a laugh.

We launched into the song again with Steven trying to keep up with 25 energetic African kids. I could tell the kids were stifling giggles at the tall mzungu man trying to dance with them. Masika couldn't hold back her laughter. She looked up at Steven and laughed out loud.

We worked on the song for another hour, recording several takes. Then it was time for lunch. Pizza was delivered, and after eating, the kids took a run around the soccer field. The chaperones hung out inside the barn, chatting with the crew. I managed to get a few moments alone with Steven.

"So how did you get involved with the choir?" he asked.

Suddenly I was more than wiling to answer the questions that I answered over and over every day.

"They performed at my church and stole my heart. When they asked for volunteers, I knew I had to go."

He smiled. "That's awesome."

I knew that my time with him was running short. I wanted to let him know what a big influence he had had on my life. I knew I'd sound like a total dork but I needed to get the words out.

"I'm so excited to meet you today I just wanted to tell you that your music has been a big influence on me and I was at one of your concerts when I decided to pursue music and I majored in music in college." I blurted out in one run on sentence.

Steven smiled, seemingly undeterred by my flustered words. "Wow, thanks for sharing that. Where'd you go to school?"

"Florida State University."

Before I had a chance to keep talking, someone came along and pulled Steven away. *Dang it.* I had also wanted to tell him how his music had led me to a more intimate relationship with Jesus. Maybe it was better that it was brief. It kept my dorkiness to a more limited dose.

After our lunch break, we returned to the set for more recording. We worked on the second song, "All I Really Want for Christmas." I listened as the kids sang and realized they were sharp. They were tired and over-stimulated. I reminded them yet again to open their mouths and to power the phrase with the breath. Steven gave them guidance as well, and I smiled as he told them some of the very same things I had instructed them on the day before in rehearsal.

"Can you sing like angels?" Steven said to them. "Make it sound pretty!" The kids looked back at me and giggled. I smiled and winked. They thought I was crazy with some of the things I would ask them to do. When they heard these same suggestions come from someone else, they were always surprised.

Even the guy recording their vocals had some pointers. "Can you sing softer and lighten up on the "yah" of Hallelujah?" he asked.

It fixed the problem. Their beautiful, angelic voices shone through.

As we wrapped up the vocal recording, they got video footage of individual children. Jolly, Kidah, and Cissy recited scripture from Isaiah. Others got dramatic, close up shots for use in the video. I watched the video monitor as Manuel's big smile and beautiful dimples filled the screen. My kids were models. I felt goose bumps creeping up on my arms.

When all of the audio and video recording was completed, the kids performed "Abataka" (a traditional African song and dance) and "Here I Am to Worship" for Steven and the crew.

They gave the kids a huge round of applause when they finished.

Feeling bold, I asked Steven for a song. He agreed, picked up his guitar, and then performed an acoustic version of "Live Out Loud." The kids danced and clapped along.

When Steven finished the song, it was time to say goodbye. The kids gave hugs to everyone and climbed onto the bus. The chaperones snuck in hugs as well, and then we followed the children onto the bus. We all waved goodbye through the windows. I settled into my bus seat and pulled out my autographed copy of Steven's latest Christmas CD. He had gifted everyone in the choir a copy including all of the chaperones. It was more than the Gaithers had done for us. I had to buy my copy of the finished album after it was released.

On the drive through the beautiful Tennessean countryside, I slipped Steven's CD into my player and lost myself in the music, thanking God for such an awesome opportunity.

~

SIX MONTHS LATER, I was listening to another demo that we were scheduled to record.

I had first seen Jars of Clay in concert in 1995 before they made it big. They opened for another act and were a little known Christian band at the time. About a year after that, they were all over the radio. Their debut self-titled album had been among my favorite Christian albums. I had been really excited when their song "Flood" was played on the secular radio station. I saw them perform several times after that first performance, including at the Creation mosh pit.

The band had reached out to us, asking the kids to perform backing vocals on their upcoming record. I had become so used to these special events that I almost forgot to be excited about it. Then I remembered I was about to work with a band that I used to fan girl over when I was sixteen.

When I found a few quiet moments alone, I slipped the demo into the CD player and sat back to listen. Sounds of a steel guitar and a steady drumbeat filled the room. Then the vocals began.

Catch the rain, empty hands
Save the children from their lands
Wash the darkness from their skin
Heroes from the West
We don't know you, we know best
But this is not a test

You treat me like I'm blind
Setting fires around houses on the hill
But light gives heat
You segregate my mind
Burning crosses from your fears
But light gives heat

I listened to the song another time, taking in the lyrics. I was a bit confused on their meaning, but I believed it alluded to Western missionaries, the way so many come to third world countries assuming they have all the right answers.

I had begun to see traces of this problem in my work with African children. I used to believe that mission work was the most noble of professions, full of brave souls who risked their lives and gave up comforts to bring the light of Christ to the most needy of people. Since my time on tour, I had begun to see how many Westerners believed they held the answer to all of life's questions. They waltzed into lives with the intent to fix all problems, even some that didn't exist. And it seemed that to the entire world, Africa was the place that needed to be fixed.

I thought of one of my recent host families. The kids had just spent an hour playing with the host family kids and were now upstairs in the shower. The host uncle turned to me and stated, "Once they return home, they must spend the rest of their lives trying to get back here."

I was a bit confused on what he meant so I asked him to clarify.

"Well, "he replied. "After they've been to America, it must be so hard to return to Africa. Once they see this, they must never want to go back!"

I swallowed, trying to decide the best way to respond. I went with gentle honesty.

"Actually, the kids are really excited to return to Africa."

He seemed genuinely surprised. "Really?"

I continued. "They're so excited to return to their homes, to their families, and to everything familiar. It's what they know and what they love. Sure, they don't have washing machines or big houses, but they don't care. Africa is their *home*."

He still seemed like he couldn't entertain the notion that someone would choose a third world country over America. I had seen this same attitude from a lot of other people in recent months. America is the best country in the world, full stop. Why would anyone possibly choose another country over the good ol' U S of A?

I couldn't get too irritated at this host uncle's statement. At one time, I had shared his sentiments. I thought I had all the right answers, that I knew the solution to every problem.

Early on my first tour, I saw the kids stuffing tin foil and saran wrap from their lunches into their school bags. I chastised them, assuming they were being lazy. I ordered them to throw away their trash. They pleaded with me to let them keep it. After a bit of arguing, I realized they were trying to save enough pieces to make a ball. With each collected piece, the size of the ball grew until it was big enough to use at playtime for dodge ball. They weren't hoarding trash. They were doing the very thing they had done their whole lives: using any and every item they had in any and every way they could. I felt guilt over the way I had yelled at them.

I thought also to a conversation I'd had with Abraham on my first tour. We walked through a neighborhood somewhere in Alaska, and he commented how America is so far ahead of Uganda in so many ways: in technology, infrastructure, buildings, and roads. But then he stopped and pointed to a sprinkler watering a lawn.

"But there are ways that Uganda is so far ahead of America. That thing," he motioned again toward the sprinkler, "keeps you from having a conversation with your neighbor as you water your lawn." He proceeded to tell me about how important community was in Uganda and the many ways that he connected with neighbors and friends. I guiltily looked at the sprinkler and thought of how seldom I had spoken with my neighbors. I also wondered how many well-intentioned missionaries had come to Uganda forcing these great technological advances onto a society that never asked for them.

Heroes from the West
We don't know you, we know best

ON THE DAY of the recording, our bus moved through the streets of downtown Nashville looking for the recording studio. As we drove along, Jessica commented, "I don't think I would even recognize them if I saw them," even though she had been a fan of Jars of Clay for years.

"I think I will," I replied. I was pretty confident in my Christian musician knowledge.

We pulled up to the building and saw a young man

standing outside. I got off the bus with Jessica and Craig and shook his hand. We found out where the kids needed to be and started unloading.

A few minutes later I learned that the man I had just shook hands with was Dan Haseltine, lead singer of Jars of Clay. And I didn't even recognize him. Jessica laughed at me for about five minutes straight.

We shuffled the kids into a cramped recording studio. I'm sure it was quite roomy for a band of four, but with a choir of twenty-five, there wasn't a lot of elbowroom. I expected Lydia to join me as we had done with the Gaithers. The kids would be singing in Luganda, and I needed help with the words. Instead, she patted me on the back, gave me a big smile, and told me I would be fine. Then, she followed the rest of the chaperones into another room before I could object. I suspected she didn't want to stuff herself into the recording studio with us. I didn't blame her. There wasn't much room left.

I looked around excitedly. The whole recording experience was still so cool to me. I loved the big bulky headphones, super sensitive microphones that picked up the faintest whisper, cords plugged into fancy equipment, and the rush of capturing music that would be played over and over for years. I was slightly nervous but mostly just excited.

The band gave some brief instructions and then played the song through the headphones so the kids had a chance to run through it. They began to sing, and I gave them their cues and tried to fake my way through the Luganda text.

The kids were tired. I could tell by the foggy look in their eyes. I could also tell by their pitch. It was really flat.

We had been going nonstop for a while, and though the kids seemed to have a never-ending supply of energy, even they had their limits. I couldn't blame them. Four concerts every week had started to wear on us. We were all exhausted. I looked at Hamisi on the back row and his slumped shoulders. His eyes blinked slowly as he tried to focus. Even Winnie, who was usually attentive during performances and rehearsals, struggled to keep her eyes on me.

I tried to encourage and energize them, putting on my goofiest of smiles. I got some smiles and giggles, but their singing was still flat. I reminded them that our camp break was only a few days away. We had a week off full of soccer playing, movie watching, and candy binging. I also reminded them that they were professional musicians. Even though they were tired, it was time to give their best. My words didn't do much to fix their pitches.

I knew that the miracle of recording equipment and auto tune could probably fix it, but I also knew that they could do better. The band assured us that it sounded fine. They could surely relate to the weariness of tour life.

Then someone in the band asked if there was anyone that would be comfortable with a solo. Jessica piped up through the headphones and suggested Elizabeth.

I smiled, knowing that Elizabeth was a strong vocalist with a sweet voice. Being Kenyan, Luganda was not her first language, but I was confident that she had learned the part well enough. She stepped forward, and with eyes glued to me, she sweetly sang the chorus.

Her voice grew stronger as she sang, gaining more confidence with each line. As she finished, the last line echoed in my ears, amplified by the microphone and the headphones that engulfed my ears.

Etala leweh bugumu...

There was a brief pause, and then I heard a voice over the headphones.

"Beautiful." It sounded like one of the band members.

Months later, we received a finished copy of the album. As I had done with the demo track, I slipped the disc into the player. Before the instruments had even begun, Elizabeth's sweet, strong voice filled the air. Chills ran down my spine. On the third chorus, the rest of the kids sang out loud and strong. For a moment, I was transported back to the recording studio. But now I didn't care about flat pitches. All I knew was that I was really proud of my kids.

19

CONCERTS AND HAIR BRAIDS

I walked slowly beside a straight line of children. Lined up outside the sanctuary door, they were decked out in bright purples and oranges. The girls' heads were wrapped in scarves and the boys' heads covered in hats. They were about to burst from the energy inside them. I walked the fine line of keeping them quiet while making sure they didn't lose the energy they needed for their performance. In less than a minute, they would be bounding onto the stage, shrieking those joyful African chants that I loved.

I walked by each child and made playful gazes at each face with my finger to my lips, reminding them to keep silent. I made crazy eyes and heard stifled giggles. I zipped my head to the left and made an overly dramatic frown. More giggles. They knew I wasn't angry, but they also knew this drill. Stay still, stay quiet, but be ready to pounce once I give the cue. Feet wiggled, and bodies convulsed. They couldn't wait to run down the aisles, shouting and startling the people sitting in the pews.

I had been on tour for two years. My original plan was to tour for one year with one choir. But once I started with my second choir, I fell in love and couldn't bear the thought of leaving.

I was tired from the constant travel, and yet this pre-concert moment still energized me. I had seen this show so many times, but it still made me happy.

I heard a muffle in my ear, and I pushed the earpiece farther in.

"Ten seconds..." Rachel whispered into her radio. I took my place at the front of the line and placed my hand on Mary's shoulder. She looked at me and grinned, then faced forward, taking her mark like a runner at the starting block.

I gave Mary the cue, and she flew down the aisle. The rest of the line followed behind her, and I shouted at each one going by.

"GO! GO! GO!" I poked playfully at a few, and Denis laughed as he dodged my finger. Clapping my hands to the beat, I continued to shout in their direction until the last child was out of the church lobby, racing their way toward the stage. They danced their way to their three choir rows on stage, hands raised high and voices chanting.

"AAAAYYYYEEEEEAAAAAAYYYYEEEE!"

Within 30 seconds, they were in place on stage and out of my hands. Rachel hit play on the first track, and the kids expertly sang and danced their way through "He Is My Light." I walked slowly along the back of the church, watching faces in the crowd as they smiled toward the stage. Knowing the kids responded better to an energetic crowd, I began to clap on the beat. Several people around me joined in, and before long the entire crowd was clapping. Sure enough, the kid's energy level began to rise.

The kids sang through each song on our program, their smiles never waning. I loved the fact that even without a single stage light on their dark faces, those smiles would still shine through. Their joy was contagious. It's why I constantly encouraged them to keep smiling.

The first half ended, and the kids danced their way off the stage. I stood in the back of the lobby, arms raised with two fingers. I didn't have to say a word. The kids made two lines in front of me: boys and girls. Once the last child was off the stage, I put my finger to my lips and motioned for them to follow. Once again, they knew the drill. Be quiet and be quick.

We arrived back at the changing rooms, and I reminded them to be fast. I entered the girls' room and watched as clothes were stripped off and tossed into piles. Fiona gave a stern look to one of the younger girls and reminded her to fold her dress neatly. Titters of laughter and voices surrounded me as they swapped stories from the first half and rifled through the suitcase for their new costume.

"Ahhh, Douglas stepped on my fooooot!"

"Eeee, Prossy, that is my skirt!"

"Eh, did you see the man dancing?"

"Carol, be fast! You are sloooow!"

I stifled my smile and shushed them. "Shhhh, girls. Dress quickly." I loved to listen to their sweet voices but knew we only had a short amount of time to change. I pushed the earpiece back into my ear and turned the volume up. We would be getting our cue to line up any minute now.

The boys had finished changing and were waiting to line up outside the girls' room. Auntie Lydia called them in and lined them into their rows. Lydia was the choir director for each concert. She and I had worked together through this last year to make sure the choir was performing at its absolute best.

"I need more energy!" Lydia said to the children. "I am falling asleep in front of you!" She mimicked herself falling asleep standing up. The kids giggled, and Lydia snapped her finger at them. "Ah! I am serious. More energy." The kids nodded in unison.

I so admired the way Lydia handled the kids. She had a stern yet loving way about her. The kids loved and respected her, and I could see the way they responded to her from the stage. I loved how she conducted them and encouraged them to perform with so much energy.

"Auntie Lydia is right," I chimed in. "You seem lazy tonight. Your sound is good, but we need more energy." Anyone sitting in the audience would have thought we were crazy asking for more energy. On their laziest days, these kids put aerobic workouts to shame. But we knew what they were capable of and didn't expect anything less.

"And Galale!" Galale's head snapped to attention. He had been fidgeting and whispering to Martha next to him.

"Yes, Auntie?"

"Keep your eyes on Auntie!" I pointed to Lydia. "I can see you keep looking away all night! Your eyes are all over. Focus, Ssebo!"

Ssebo is Lugandan for *sir*. The kids snapped to attention more when I spoke their languages, even if just one or two words.

Galale smiled sheepishly and said, "Yes, Auntie."

"Two minutes..." I heard in my earpiece.

"Alright, everyone line up!" The kids scurried quickly to their place. Within a minute, we were lined up outside the sanctuary again, ready to start the second half. We went through the same routine as the beginning of the concert; they stood quietly in line while their little bodies practically shook from the energy bottled inside them, waited for my cue, and then once again barreled onto the stage.

I found a secluded pew in the back, notebook and pen propped on my knee. I looked toward the stage and watched the kids dance. Their voices blared through the speakers. I glanced around and saw people smiling, some heads bopped back and forth to the beat. It was hard to sit still during their shows. A couple small children moved toward the stage and mimicked the movement before them. I smiled at their small flailing arms and their feet struggling to keep up with the motions.

I looked down at my notebook and jotted a couple notes.

Need more consistent vowels. Work on rounding their vowels, opening mouth more.

Pitch going flat in "Teach Me to Dance." Work on breath support.

Abataka: movements not together.

The concert was winding to a close. The choir began their second to last song, "Walking in the Light." I put the cap on my pen and closed my notebook. Sometimes I spent so much time taking notes, so focused on the things to fix, that I missed the joy and energy of this show. Every few concerts, I made a conscious effort to put my notebook aside and just enjoy the show.

"Walking in the Light" was one of the highlights of the performance. It was based on the song "This Little Light of Mine." The audience enjoyed the familiar words, and the energy of the song was contagious. Even the most quiet of audiences was driven to its feet, clapping and cheering. This was my favorite song to sit back and take in.

I laughed out loud as Joash grabbed the mic. He had only been singing the solo for a few weeks, but he was definitely amping up the energy and his stage presence. I had watched him practice new dance moves in his spare time: on the playground and in host families. We encouraged him to improv and get the audience into the song. Every night it was a new move, and every show his confidence grew. It made my heart happy to see him with such a huge grin, moving and shaking in ways I never could. And his voice. It had grown from light and airy to full and confident. He owned that stage, and I was so proud.

The crowd was definitely into it, a few people clapping, everyone smiling. But I knew the best moment was yet to come. This was the moment that I most loved to watch the crowd's reaction.

"Ladies and gentleman," Joash bellowed into the mic. "The African... Children's... CHOOOOOOOOIIIIIRRRRRRR!!!!!" He shouted the last line and returned the mic to its stand and then danced his way back to his place in the choir.

The audience jumped to their feet, cheering loudly in approval. The applause was deafening.

The rest of the kids fed off Joash's energy, and the instrumental dance interlude began. They moved with the energy that Lydia and I had encouraged during the break. As they danced, they shouted loudly. "Hey HEY! Ho HO!!!"

Back and forth their little feet pounded the wood floor beneath them, jumping high and grinning big. The crowd around me clapped along loudly, many still cheering or whistling.

"Walking into the light!"

The kids' hands shot up high on their final line, the track stopped, and the stage lights went black. The audience again erupted into cheers. They would have given a standing ovation if they weren't already standing. My heart swelled. I was proud of the way these kids energized each and every crowd, week after week.

The pastor came on stage, prayed a short prayer, and asked the kids to do one more song, which of course they always did. The track began for "Oh Happy Day," and I watched proudly as Moses took the mic for the solo. Like Joash, his confidence had skyrocketed since performing the solo. He also threw in a few new dance moves, inspiring the audience to clap along.

As the encore wound to a close, I went to my usual position with two fingers in the air. The kids came flying into the lobby and immediately formed two lines. I put a finger to my lips, reminding them to quiet down. I knew it was a futile effort, near impossible to expect them to plunge into silence after their energetic performance. But it at least brought the volume down from shouts to tittered whispers.

I gave them a big grin, and they smiled back. With the end of one more concert, I led them back to their changing rooms. The kids would change, pack up their (smelly) concert clothes, and wait for their new host families to gather and take them home.

Once Auntie Lydia was in the changing room (she often got stopped by audience members raving about the performance), I returned to the sanctuary to coil microphone cords and carry sound equipment back to the bus. As I scurried around, I would hear people gush about how wonderful the children were.

"So much energy!"

"Such a beautiful sound!"

Sometimes people would stop me and speak these words of praise to my face. Other times, they would be oblivious to my presence, standing on top of the cord I was trying to pack away. This was always the time of the night where exhaustion set in. The energy of the concert less than 20 minutes before was already fading away, and my patience was wearing thin. Even those times when people would stop me and thank me for my work with the kids, I wished they would go away so I could pack up quicker. I appreciated their words though, so as tired as I was, I would plaster on a smile and thank them.

After everything was packed away, it was time to meet our host families. Night after night, I met the kind strangers that would take me to their home and let me sleep in their bed. This particular night the fatigue was sinking in quickly, and I prayed for a kind family, one that would recognize how exhausted we all were and might give us a few moments of quiet without the usual questions.

I got that wish. Our host family gave us a small snack of popcorn, hugged us, and bid us goodnight. They left me alone to get the girls ready for bed. I prayed a silent prayer of thanks.

Mwikali was in the shower. I could hear her singing through the door. Lying on the bed, I lazily stared at the ceiling while Rebecca braided my hair into tiny little braids. Lillian sat on the double bed with us and talked a mile a minute, recounting story after story about life in Uganda. She told me about her family, how she had to fetch water for cooking, and about her long walk to school. Rebecca chimed in on a few stories with an excited, "Yes, Auntie!" as she herself launched into stories about how it was at home in Kenya.

The girls asked me for stories of my home, and I told them a few about my family. They enjoyed hearing stories about my nephews, especially the baby, Aidan. They giggled at my jokes, and Rebecca began yet another braid.

Mwikali came out of the shower and saw the hair appointment happening without her. She dropped her clothes on the floor then jumped onto the bed. She grabbed a section of hair and began to braid along with Rebecca.

"Eeee, Auntie, your hair will not stay," Mwikali said as she finished her first braid. The kids grew irritated at the way my smooth hair wouldn't hold a braid. As soon as they let go, the strands would unwrap themselves. I often offered them hair bands, but I never had enough for the dozens of braids they would make.

Lillian rifled through her bag, still talking. She found a comb and came over to the bed. She began to pull it gently through my hair. I now had three hairdressers.

I knew I should be urging Lillian or Rebecca to get in the shower.

It was late and I was supposed to be getting these girls ready for bed. But this moment was too special to rush through. I only had a few months left with these kids, and I wanted to soak up every moment, especially moments like this one.

Five more minutes, I told myself as Rebecca began another braid.

20

PAINFUL WORSHIP

The dreaded day had arrived. It was time to send my kids back home. My second choir had completed its tour, and in less than eight hours, my kids would be getting on an airplane bound for Africa. I thought back to my last day with my first choir, and I knew this goodbye wouldn't be any easier.

We woke up and went through the motions, packing bags and putting things on the bus. I handed out homemade cards for my kids, and they gratefully accepted them. Many of them gave me letters with carefully printed English and beautiful, colorful pictures. I packed them away to read later when I was alone with a box of Kleenex.

During lunch, everyone was oddly quiet. We all knew what was coming, and none of us knew what to say. After lunch, we gathered into one last devotions circle.

We decided to let everyone lead one song. We got halfway around the circle, and I realized that today devotions was simply draining me. I usually loved this time with my kids, my blessed aunties and uncles, my family, but knowing that this was the last one was so emotionally exhausting I almost couldn't take it. With the start of each song, I thought to myself, "I can't do this anymore." I wanted to curl up in the corner and cry. Instead, I put on a smile and kept singing, trying to ignore the stinging tears that threatened to pour down my face.

Someone began to sing "Blessed Be Your Name." The kids had recently learned it, and it came up often in our devotion song lineup. The kids raised their hands high as they sang.

> *You give and take away*
> *You give and take away*
> *My heart will choose to say*
> *Lord blessed be Your name*

I could barely get the words out.

God, That's exactly what you're doing here. You gave me these beautiful children and now you're taking them back. No fair!

Internally, I stuck my tongue out at God.

In that circle, my heart was not choosing to say, "blessed be Your name." I wanted to cross my arms in front of my chest and stomp my feet. As I stood there in one of the last precious moments with my kids, I wasn't feeling too fond of God. I wanted to scream at God and fall on the floor and kick my feet and wave my arms like an infant throwing a tantrum. The last thing I felt like doing was worshiping God. I was angry with Him for taking my kids away. Even though I knew it was something I had to do, I hated it.

I loved those kids with everything I had. For almost three years, I had poured my heart into these choirs. I had already faced one painful goodbye, and now I had to do it again. These kids had become such an important part of my life. How was I supposed to go through life without them?

I wasn't ready to let them go. I wanted tour life to go on. I wanted to spend the rest of my days with these kids, teaching them songs and playing soccer and having my hair braided.

But that couldn't happen. They had to go home. As much as it sucked, I knew it was coming.

As I stood in that circle, it took everything in me to sing the words, "My heart will choose to say, Lord, blessed be Your name..." I wasn't in full agreement with that statement, but I knew I would get there eventually.

That day was my first real lesson in the fact that worship does not always feel good. Standing in our devotions circle, the worship hurt. I felt my heart ripping in two in anticipation of the goodbye to come.

I wasn't the only one who was feeling emotionally wrenched. Everyone else was half-heartedly singing too. We eventually gave up and shared testimonies: small snippets of gratitude.

"I thank God that He has brought us here safely."

"I thank God that I will see my family again soon."

"I thank God for our aunties and uncles."

I choked up as Alex shared that last one. On and on the testimonies went as we shared good memories and stories from tour. We thanked God for all He had done for us. My heart softened slightly.

Hours later, my heart hardened again, and snot dripped out of my nose.

The only other time I had cried this hard was a year and a half ago when I walked away from my first group of kids. Now, I stood in the middle of the London Heathrow Airport, having just hugged my second group of kids for the last time. Huddled among my group of fellow aunties and uncles, we clutched each other and sobbed as the last 15 months of our lives walked away toward a plane headed home.

After a couple minutes, we pulled ourselves together as best as we could. I was still sobbing and gasping for air. We walked toward the bathroom and received more than a few weird stares.

Sharye, one of my fellow chaperones, managed to eke out between tears, "If we run, we can get them back!" I, too, was stifling the urge to fight through the crowd and pull my kids back into my arms.

But we knew we couldn't. A season was ending. It was time for our children to return home and so should we. As we neared the restroom door, I turned around, sadly looking at the lack of baby ducklings on my tail. Only 30 minutes before, I had led my line of kids to this same bathroom.

Standing in front of the mirror, Jessica looked at me and said, "You look like crap!"

I looked back at her. "You look worse!" We both laughed, but even that mere act was exhausting. Our laughs faded away, the sound echoing off the tile wall, reminders of the last year of happy memories. I sighed, grabbed my stained backpack, and trudged out the door. That baby blue Jansport had seen more than its fair share of adventure. I think even it was sad that the kids were gone.

We stopped for some medicinal Starbucks (just holding my cup gave me comfort) and ambled our way toward the train. We sat for at least an hour, not saying anything. None of us had the energy. I leaned my head against the window as a few more tears slid down my cheek.

When I was absolutely done and felt like I couldn't take another step, we walked through the door of the London house where we would stay for the next few days. We had all made a mutual decision to spend a few days together before going our separate ways. We set our luggage down then just sat and stared at each other. None of us had any idea what to do. I felt helpless, purposeless.

I plopped onto a couch and stared at nothing. I thought back to the song we had sung earlier in that tight knit circle.

My heart will choose to say...

No, I still wasn't ready for that. In that moment, my heart chose to pout.

After staring into space for several minutes, I shuffled into the computer room and sat down in front of a monitor. I stared at the screen for a minute then logged into my e-mail. I sent an e-mail to Drew, a friend from home.

> *Hi Drew. My head is pounding, my eyes are bloodshot, and I feel numb. My babies are gone. It was a rough goodbye in the airport... Oh, that was a hard moment when they walked away. We all just stood there and sobbed for a few minutes after. I'm sure we created quite the scene.*
>
> *Thanks for your prayers. See you in a week or two.*
>
> *Jamie*

The computer dinged a few moments later, signaling Drew's quick response.

> *Thanks for sharing...*
>
> **hugs* drew*

I wondered if he knew how much that simple response meant to me. I wasn't looking for comfort or answers. I simply needed to share that the current moment in my life totally sucked. He acknowledged that.

With my limited energy, the only response I could give was:

> *Sure. I'm going to go finish my Starbucks and wander aimlessly some more...*

I was still staring at the computer screen when his next response came through.

> *Not aimless, just looking for the next phase of your purpose...*

PART VII

DISSONANCE

21

DON'T DO, JUST BE

After spending a few days in the London house, I joined Jessica and Sharye for a quick trip to Holland. Jessica had family there, and they graciously let me stay with them. I enjoyed those days with my fellow chaperones. It was nice to be with people who were grieving the same loss that I was, that understood how sad I felt. We explored the countryside of Holland, admired the windmills, and visited museums. But after a week, I was weary and ready to return home. I hugged Jessica and Sharye tightly as I left for the airport. I didn't know when I might see them again, but I knew we had formed a lifelong friendship.

I flew back across the Atlantic Ocean, alone once again. With my head propped against the double pane window, gazing out at clouds and endless miles of water, I thought back to another transatlantic flight. Three years before, I had flown to Uganda all alone. I smiled to myself as I remembered how my heart had been pumping on that flight. My smile faltered as I thought about how much had changed.

When I returned home, nothing felt the same. College friends had moved away finding jobs in other towns. Church had gone through a variety of changes. My dad had begun a job in a new city, and my parents were in the process of moving from the house I had lived in since I was nine years old. I was home, but it sure didn't feel like it.

I was so drained from the last three years that all I wanted to do was curl up in bed. There was physical exhaustion for sure, but that didn't compare to the mental and emotional exhaustion I was trying to overcome. I was grieving the loss of my kids, and my brain was trying desperately to catch up.

I went to church, plastering on a smile for the sake of those around me. People asked about my time with the African Children's Choir, but they only wanted the five-second answer.

"Great! Totally life changing!"

Most people didn't want to stick around to hear how when I closed my eyes, I could still hear the sweet voices of my children singing Luganda worship songs. How my arms ached to receive my daily allotment of twenty-five little hugs. How much I missed tucking my kids in at night. How even though it had been three years since I had been there, I could still see the dust rising from the Kampala streets and hear the call to prayer from the building down the street each morning when I woke.

If anyone did want to stick around to hear more, I didn't know where to start and usually went with the easy answer anyway. It's hard to sum up such an experience, and some days I just didn't have the energy to talk about it.

I took a lot of long walks, silently strolling through forest trails, sorting through my thoughts and trying to figure out what was next.

Fitting back into "normal" life was incredibly difficult. Even worship was hard. What had once been so effortless and fulfilling was now draining. I didn't want to stand on the front row, hands raised. I stood in the back of the room instead. I longed for a small, tight-knit circle and African drums. Worship from the stage didn't reach me like it once had. Members of the praise band urged me to return to the stage. I politely declined.

One Sunday, three months after returning home, I hid in the back and listened to the song playing from the stage.

> *Lead me to the cross where your love*
> *poured out*
> *Bring me to my knees, Lord I lay me down*
> *Rid me of myself, I belong to You*
> *Oh lead me, lead me to the cross*

Just three short years before, these words would have moved me. I would have stood speechless in that sanctuary, tears biting the corners of my eyes and my soul full to the brim. Now those words seemed empty. Hollow. Meaningless.

The electric guitar solo blared through the speakers. People raised their hands high above their heads while I stared downward at mine, wringing nervously at my stomach. I heard a "Hallelujah!" from a few rows in front of me.

I felt like an outsider, like I was the only one who wasn't getting it. Everyone around me was in this club, totally connected to God and one another, and I was wondering when I got kicked out. I was left standing outside, staring through the window while my grubby hands left fingerprints all over the glass.

I began to realize how contemporary musical worship had been my personal idol. It was the musical high, the warm fuzzies, the elusive happy and full feeling that I would experience each Sunday morning. It was a hit of adrenaline, and I relished in it each week, throwing my head back and thanking God for being fully present.

Now that I wasn't experiencing the warm fuzzies, I felt like worship wasn't real. And once I realized I had been chasing the high all those years, I wondered how much of my worship had been really genuine.

I thought back to when I started on tour and how much I missed worship at home. I wanted acoustic guitars and music stands and "How Great is Our God." But as tour continued on and became the norm of life, devotions became my worship time. Now I couldn't see worshipping (at least musically) any other way.

As I stood empty before the stage, I longed for one more devotion circle with my kids. I missed that time more than I could say, missed my kids tugging on my sleeve and then whispering into my ear the meaning of the Luganda and Swahili songs.

Devotions took the form of true worship in my heart. It was hard to stand and worship before a stage now. That sort of worship now felt forced and overly produced. Worship felt more natural, more real when I stood in a circle of my favorite people, people that I was doing this messy thing called life with, those people that I loved so dearly.

I realized that church was supposed to be exactly that: a beautiful, messy place, where we do life together. A place filled with broken people just like me. Musical worship was the time for all of us to offer up our voices and blend into the sea of worshippers around us. I believed there was beauty to be found in that church sanctuary, surrounded by people singing along to contemporary worship. But no matter how hard I tried, I couldn't seem to find it.

I longed for the tug on my shirt-sleeve and the sweet whisper into my ear so I could understand.

~

I STRUGGLED with more than worship. All of faith became a struggle. Bible reading and prayer were only stale things on the to-do list. I knew God was still there, but all the things in my walk that had been so sure were suddenly hazy.

Church became a chore. I made myself go, mainly for community. I knew community was important, and I wanted to keep engaging. As an introvert (and socially anxious person), I knew how all too easy it was to disappear into myself. I had a tendency to disappear so deeply that I would end up wallowing in every bad emotion that festered under the surface of my fake smile. Community would give me a place to process those ugly feelings and remind me of the beauty of humanity.

So I kept forcing myself out of bed every Sunday morning. But instead of getting easier, it got harder. It didn't help that a dear friend had been deeply hurt by our church. She was passive-aggressively forced out of her employment as worship leader and left intensely scarred by the one place where she should have been most safe. Seeing her so badly bruised left me feeling even more tender. To make matters worse, she was the second friend who had been left traumatized after being fired from her church job. I was confused by the church politics and drama surrounding me. The more I tried to participate at church, the more my resentments slowly reared their ugly heads.

I felt empty. With each passing day, my post tour life felt meaningless.

I would find out later that this is normal for missionaries coming off the field. There's a weird transition period where your old normal is uncomfortable. Even though I had spent the majority of my time in America, I still felt out of place at home, like I didn't fit anymore.

Emily, my fellow African Children's Choir chaperone from my first choir that I had quickly befriended in Uganda, came for a visit. Even after I left for my second choir, we had kept in regular contact. Our time together on tour had solidified the bond between us, and we knew that we were best friends for life, even though we lived on opposite sides of the country.

We spent time drinking coffee, journaling, reliving tour memories, and driving aimlessly down canopy roads, streets entirely covered by oak branches with moss dripping from each bough. Emily fell in love with these roads and affectionately dubbed them "droopy branches."

Being with someone who was experiencing the same emotions was incredibly comforting. I didn't need to vocalize my feelings; I knew she felt the same way. Which was good, because my feelings were such a jumbled mess that I didn't know how to express them.

We went to see a woman who counsels missionaries coming off the field. My pastor had recommended her, and I figured talking through some things would be helpful. If nothing else, it would be wonderful to have a captive audience so I could talk about my kids.

The visit was a blur. I was uncomfortable opening up to a complete stranger. I had no experience with any kind of counseling or small group settings before that. When I teared up, I refused to let the emotions take over and instead, swallowed the lump in my throat. I was too full of pride to let myself be completely vulnerable.

What I do remember about that visit is one phrase: "Don't do. Just be."

Emily and I shared how frustrating quiet time and church had become. How empty it felt. We would try to pray or read our obligatory Bible reading for the day, and it didn't feel like it used to feel. We were just going through the motions, and neither of us liked that. The counselor smiled in understanding.

"Stop trying to do things. It's like a little child that just wants to sit in Daddy's lap. That child is just enjoying her father's presence. Just like that, you need to be with God, and stop trying to do. Don't do... just be."

These words of wisdom made sense. We had been doing so much through our time on tour. Tour was a constant whirlwind of activity with very little downtime. Now that our lives were full of downtime, we didn't know how to act.

The more I thought about it, the more these words made sense. I put so much focus on the things I should do that I left my soul crazy. I longed for stillness but couldn't achieve it.

When I attended church worship, I felt like I was supposed to feel certain things or act a specific way. When really, I just needed to be fully present.

I needed to stop worrying about the people around me, stop guilt-tripping myself for not reading the Bible as much as I "should," and stop feeling like I needed butterflies and warm fuzzies during worship for it to be real.

Don't do. Just be. These words continued to haunt me for months.

22

MY MUSICAL COMING OF AGE

Shortly after tour ended, my love story began. Drew and I had known each other for five years. We had worked on the praise team together, me as a vocalist and he running sound and graphics. We can't remember exactly when we first met, but we both remember one thing: we didn't really like each other.

You'd be hard-pressed to think of two people less likely to be together. In my eyes, he was a coarse, crude, beer-swilling heathen. In his eyes, I was a prissy, stuck-up, goody-two-shoes church girl.

Turns out we were both right.

Fast-forward five years. We had both gone through lots of life changes. He had done a lot of soul searching throughout his divorce, and I had slowly begun the descent from my holy high horse. But still, neither of us would have entertained the notion that something might happen between us.

I was home for a short break before returning for my last few months of tour. Drew approached me at church as I stood visiting with several friends. He stood to the side, waiting patiently for the conversation to subside. I vaguely noticed him. I was busy laughing and hugging all those around me.

I hugged the last of my friends and turned to Drew. I craned my neck to look up at him. At 6'5", he towered above me. He gave me his signature mischievous grin. "You are absolutely crazy to go back on tour."

I just smiled back, knowing how so few people could understand the passion I had for the ministry and the kids involved in it. Rather than attempting to address his statement, I changed the subject.

"Thanks for your support while I've been away." He had given a little money when I started my tour journey, and I knew he had kept up with my newsletter updates.

"It's the least I can do. Literally," he replied with another grin and a small laugh.

I figured that I would say goodbye and then return home to start my laundry and packing. But then he invited me to lunch with him and a couple friends. I accepted.

As we wrapped up our Chinese buffet lunch a couple hours later, I cracked open my fortune cookie and laughed out loud at the slip of paper that fell into my hands. "The time is right for a friendly chat to lead to romance."

"Oooo," Drew teased. "Maybe you'll meet some guy on the road."

I rolled my eyes. "Not likely. We're never in one place long enough."

Drew made a couple more bantering remarks about the fortune. I rolled my eyes again, but then I took out my wallet and put the fortune inside. I liked this one and wanted to hang onto it.

They paid for lunch, and we walked outside. I gave Drew a quick hug, thanked him for lunch (he had paid for mine after jokingly referring to me as a starving missionary), said goodbye to his friends, and then I left.

I had already forgotten about the fortune tucked into my wallet. I didn't look back or give a second thought to that lunch for months. It wasn't until six months later that I would find out what transpired after I left.

As I climbed into my car and drove away, Drew's friend Brian turned to him. "Dude. She's totally into you. You need to follow up with that."

Drew looked at Brian in surprise and laughed. "*Jamie*? No way."

Brian shook his head. "No, seriously. Follow up with that."

"How am I going to follow up with that? She's leaving town again. Probably moving to Africa or something."

"Send her an e-mail. Do something, dude. Keep in touch."

Brian kept insisting. Drew finally promised to send me an e-mail, and the conversation drifted to other topics I'm not privy to.

Years later, I teased Brian about that comment as I was not into Drew at all. He just shook his head and replied, "I saw something. Maybe it wasn't attraction, but it was something."

I'm so glad he did. Without that comment, my love story might not have happened.

DREW DID SEND THAT EMAIL. When I responded, he sent another. And then another. We ended up emailing consistently throughout my last six months of tour. I didn't think much of it. I was thankful for some regular correspondence to someone at home. He was not my type, so I didn't even entertain the thought of it leading anywhere.

Still, Drew gave me an open invitation to get together once I returned home from tour. He wanted to show me the movie *Groundhog Day*. He had alluded to the movie in our emails after I talked about how life on tour was always the same questions and conversations over and over. When I confessed I had never seen the movie, he declared that we needed to remedy that. He threw dinner into the deal, and I took him up on his offer.

I didn't think about the fact that the evening was awfully date-like until I was on my way there. It honestly hadn't even occurred to me. I was just looking forward to a night with a friend. Was he expecting more?

I peeked into the rearview and saw my makeup-less face and tired eyes. I had thrown my hair into a messy ponytail to go with my old, faded jeans and hoodie sweatshirt. I was not looking sexy, which was pretty much the message I was trying to convey.

I apprehensively knocked on the door, unsure of what Drew's expectations were. He answered the door wearing a shirt that read, "100% USDA Grade A Beef." I burst out laughing when I saw it.

"I made it in college!" he proudly declared. It diffused all of the tension I had begun to feel.

He made a delicious dinner of grilled salmon and steamed veggies. After dinner, we watched the movie *Must Love Dogs* because he couldn't find the Netflix disc for *Groundhog Day*. I sat on the recliner, and he sat several feet away on the love seat. When the movie was over, we talked. I told stories of my kids and how much I missed them, and he spoke of some of the concerts he had attended in the last year. Before we knew it, it was almost midnight.

"Whoa!" he said. "Time to kick you out. I have work tomorrow."

I looked at the clock. "Wow. I didn't realize it was so late." I stood up and grabbed my keys. "Thanks again for dinner."

I assumed that would be it, but then he invited me over again the next week. Since I still hadn't seen *Groundhog Day*, he wanted a second chance to show me. I didn't expect to repeat the first evening's events. I assumed that long conversation had simply been an exception. Any future conversations would surely end up awkward.

But the next week, I again walked out of his duplex a few minutes before midnight.

In addition to these dinner dates, the emails continued. I found myself looking for excuses to check my email. A week after that second dinner, Drew asked if I would like to officially date. I honestly still did not see it going anywhere but agreed to try it anyway.

I fell faster than I expected. The beer-swilling heathen had a lot more in common with the goody two shoes than we thought.

Three months into our relationship, I was cleaning out my purse. I turned my wallet upside down to empty out a few pieces of lint. A small slip of paper fluttered to the ground. I knelt down to pick it up and squinted at the small words.

"The time is right for a friendly chat to lead to romance."

The memories of that lunch came flooding back to me. The Chinese buffet, the crab rangoons, Drew's gentle teasing about the fortune.

We were engaged eight months later.

~

A YEAR BEFORE ME, Drew had dated another woman. She was a football fan, something Drew is not. Every year, she bought season tickets to the college football games. As he considered the possibility of pursuing a longer-term relationship, he thought about the fact that he would rather go to concerts than football games. He told his friend Karen that if his girlfriend would spend money on football surely he could spend money on concert tickets. He figured it was a fair compromise.

Karen looked him straight in the eye and responded, "Or you could find someone that enjoys concerts."

One of the biggest connections Drew and I have is music. We haven't been to a single football game but have been to many concerts. Lifehouse, Anberlin, and The Avett Brothers are among the bands we have seen live.

While planning our honeymoon, Drew found out that Demon Hunter, one of his favorite bands, was going to be in Atlanta the weekend we would be there.

He commented, "Man, too bad we can't go see them."

I looked at him. "Why can't we?"

"I'm not going to drag you to that on our honeymoon," he replied.

Demon Hunter is a hard-rock, screamo band. Just listening to screamo singing hurts my classically-trained vocal cords, and I was glad that he recognized that. But he had played some of their music around me, and I found Demon Hunter intriguing. I began to understand how powerful screamo singing could be and the type of training it must involve. I also loved their tight harmonies. Demon Hunter technically falls under the classification of Christian music, but it was definitely not the kind that had surrounded me for so many years.

I put my hand on Drew's arm. "And I'm not going to start our marriage by making you miss one of your favorite bands. Buy tickets."

So on our honeymoon, we walked into The Masquerade in Atlanta, Georgia. Loud, blaring guitars and grating vocals filled the air around us. As we walked inside and the screaming from other bands surrounded me, I flashed back to Jesus-freak Jamie. It sounded like Satan himself was singing.

For a brief moment, I began to regret my willingness to attend this concert. But after we settled into our space by the bar and I stuffed earplugs into my ear canals, I found I really enjoyed the show. I liked watching the energy the guitarists played with and the way the vocalist head-banged in between each verse. And I giggled when one of the opening bands declared to the audience, "If you know this one, sing along!" and then proceeded to scream his way through the verse.

Drew returned the favor from that concert. In the first years of our marriage I took him to see Andrew Peterson, Shane and Shane, and Derek Webb. And like me with Demon Hunter, he found things to enjoy in my music.

Our musical tastes differ. While I tend to drift toward quieter, more contemplative acoustic music, he thrives mostly on loud, heavy rock. What I have found in our relationship is that we've encouraged each other to consider music that is outside of our wheelhouse, which is something I desperately needed.

I had spent so much time trapped in my CCM bubble, and I didn't know how to get out. Drew helped open my eyes to a lot of other music, much of which I would never have considered on my own. When I confessed to him that I wanted to listen to music other than CCM, he went to the used music store and bought a stack of CDs for me. He bought me a variety of artists: Seal, Natalie Merchant, and The Fray.

He exposed me to bands like Metallica (they were the epitome of evil bands to avoid) and Alice in Chains. He even introduced me to rap, a genre I never would have considered on my own.

Although I still have not seen *8 Mile* in its entirety (I always catch it toward the end), I was amazed when I watched the freestyle rap scene. The musicians took a beat and created lyrics out of thin air. I was impressed at their talent and creativity. I had always assumed rap was boring music and crass lyrics. I never realized the thought and effort that went into those words and the social commentary they contained.

One genre that Drew and I had a common interest in was 90s alternative. He enjoyed the hard rock music, and for me, it was a nostalgic trip back to my teenage years. As I began to open my life to different music styles, I felt comfortable reintroducing this music back into my life. I was surprised at how many songs I recognized and how many bands I remembered. And I made Drew laugh when I busted out my best Eddie Vedder impression.

I remembered the guilt I felt for listening to these songs in high school. As I listened to the music 12 years later, it brought to mind some other feelings. Aspiration. Longing. The more I listened, the more I remembered feeling really connected to this music. I may not have fully understood the lyrics but I could identify with the passion with which they were sung. These albums were anthems to my teenage soul.

I felt pangs of regret for the CDs I had sold when I cleansed my collection. Live, Bush, Goo Goo Dolls, even Alanis Morissette... I missed them. I found something surprising in those songs. They stirred my soul. The depth of the lyrics and intense music impressed me.

I flashed back to high school, riding in my friend's cars. "Machinehead" by Bush is playing on the radio, and we're singing along, making up half the words as we go. We laugh at the ridiculous phrases we come up with. Then, I flashed back to the foothills of that Maine mountain, singing along to Nine Inch Nails at the top of my lungs and dancing with my friends. There was a time when this music energized me, a time before I let the guilt overtake me.

In addition to '90s alternative, I began to listen to other music as well. The folk genre especially spoke to me. The soft beauty in these songs beckoned to me. They were simple, unassuming, and powerful. Acoustic guitar, hammered dulcimer, banjo, and mandolin all became favorite instruments. I remembered my host auntie from Madison, Wisconsin and her musician friends that gave me a concert in her living room. I thought of the guitars and fiddles and funny drums they played and how their music made my head buzz with happiness.

I eagerly jumped onto the Mumford & Sons' bandwagon.

Groups like these showed me the passion within music, the passion I had lost in recent months. I didn't even flinch at the word *fuck* in their song "Little Lion Man." Instead, I sang along with gusto. I thought back to Tim and that Pink Floyd CD—if he could only see me now.

I listened to big band music, growing to love the CD collection that I inherited when my grandfather passed away over 10 years before. I enviously listened to Ella Fitzgerald's deep, beautiful alto voice as she effortlessly dipped down to reach the low notes, her sexy, throaty voice bellowing through the speakers.

I even reintroduced myself to classical music. I hummed along to the piano sonatas or orchestral wonders, some familiar pieces and others that I had never heard. I thought back to my years at the school of music, and it finally clicked. No wonder my voice teachers got so frustrated with me. This music was gorgeous. How could I have missed out on the wonder of singing these pieces? I heard the intricacies of the chords, the deep and rich tone of the vocalists, the wide range of instruments used. I loved that the pieces were unpredictable. The melodies that Mozart and Beethoven crafted were painfully beautiful. I listened in envy as the soprano soared high on the notes of "Panis Angelicus" and wished I had better cherished the opportunity I had to perform these works.

As I listened to a wide range of genres, I was more than a little shocked to find that non-Christian music was beautiful. There was feeling and thought that went into each song. Why did I assume all this music was bad? As I went through my musical coming of age, I began to critique the musical genre that had dominated most of my 20s. And the more that I critiqued, the more I began to wonder why I had enjoyed it so much.

23

CHRISTIAN MUSIC SUCKS

"Why are churches performing this mediocre music?" Nine years after my time at the Florida State College of Music, Dr. Wingate's question once again came to mind.

After listening to so many other music styles, I came back to CCM and listened with a more discerning ear. I had played guitar for 10 years, and I now noticed the repetitive chord structures. I picked up on clichéd, monotonous lyrics. Every song sounded the same.

The music that captivated my life for so many years became trite and trivial. Simply put, Christian music started to suck.

It was a year into my marriage when I started to make these realizations. As the months went on, I found more connection with secular songs than Christian songs.

One night, Drew and I listened to the '90s alternative Pandora station and Blues Traveler's "Hook" came on. I had heard the song many times throughout high school but had never really listened to it. That day I paid attention to the lyrics.

The song was a commentary on unoriginal music. As long as there was some catchy hook, it didn't matter what the song said. "Hook" wasn't referring specifically to Christian music, yet I couldn't help but apply the message to the music I had soundtracked my life with. The catchy hooks of CCM didn't say anything of substance but because it sounded cool it felt spiritual.

I noticed how many contemporary worship songs were focused on the hook. I began to feel uncomfortable with some of the songs we sang in church. We weren't really saying anything with our words. We were singing repetitive, catchy riffs that made our souls feel full.

In a world where three-chord songs reign, it was hard to find church music that contained real musical depth. I wanted songs that were written in something other than the key of C or D and contained more than major chords. I longed for lyrics that made me think. I grew tired of repetitive choruses, the same phrase sung over and over. I longed for more complexity.

I began to ask questions. Was this industry spoon-feeding us what we were "supposed" to hear? Why did they give us the same easy songs over and over again? Why were they trying to compact our God into three chords?

The more I dug into this, the more I realized how commercialized the industry was. CCM was marketing, plain and simple. The Christian faith is complex, but I preferred simple. I wanted easy, black and white music and messages. Why think when I could be told what to believe? Why struggle with the difficult words of Jesus when I could just proclaim, "Hallelujah!" and call it a day?

So that's what CCM gave me. Easy music. Easy theology. I sang repetitive phrases ad nauseam until they sunk so deep into my soul that it chiseled away at the real meat of my faith.

Just as I had become angry at the discovery of church politics, I became enraged at the idea that I had been strung along by a marketing scheme for so long. I began to detest Christian music. I had so much resentment. I felt lied to. Manipulated. Brainwashed.

It felt like a really nasty breakup. And once I broke free of my controlling ex-boyfriend, my music tastes began to spread even more.

I changed my radio dial and discovered blissful variety. Even though the pop/rock/country stations also had simple and often repetitive songs, they felt different somehow. I finally felt free from the self-imposed musical chains I had wrapped around myself. Every song didn't have to be about God. When I did turn back to K Love or some other Christian station, I never stayed long.

One day shortly after my thirty-second birthday, I sat in my car and listened to a Christian song blare from my speakers. I can't remember what the song was; they had all begun to run together. I felt nothing as I listened to the words. The music did not move me. I lifted my hand to the radio and deleted the station from my presets. After a couple years of musical exploration, I was officially done with Christian music.

I had found other music that carried so much depth and honesty and beauty that it made me want to cry every time I heard it. There were songs that moved me immensely, and they had nothing to do with God.

I heard Sia's "Breathe Me" and was struck by the rawness and honesty of the lyrics. What was interesting is that they were almost like a prayer. Maybe she was praying. The song drew me in with its vulnerability and helplessness. It felt more honest than many of the CCM songs that were on the radio.

In much the same way I was drawn to more complex music, I was also drawn to a deeper, more complex faith, a faith so complex it didn't feel like it was welcome in CCM culture. In that world, it felt like everything needed to be wrapped up neatly with no room for big questions. I felt that asking questions or expressing doubts was not welcome. In other music, I found a place to explore those questions. I felt stuck in CCM music. There was no place to grow. Simply stay here and trust.

Some days, I would feel pangs of guilt for the new music I introduced to my life. I guess it was that remnant of the Christian safety net I had created. It kept trying to pull me back in. It's hard to shake habits that you've held for so long.

Then, I would listen to the beauty of the secular songs again. Surely God was in this somehow, even if the words didn't specifically mention Him. Songs like Dan Rodriguez's "AWOL Hearts" and "Mad World" sung by Gary Jules; they made my heart ache in a really good way. The way you feel when you want to cry over the beauty of humanity, those times when you realize how powerful music and art and creativity are. I was reminded strongly of that feeling one October Saturday evening in 2010.

I had been feeling mopey, defeated, and overwhelmed all day, largely from trying to process through my frustration at worship music. I tried all day to pull myself out of my funk with no luck. Drew recognized my mood and decided we should go out for dinner and a drive. After dinner, we drove in the twilight with the windows down, the glow of the setting sun slinking into the horizon. *Prairie Home Companion* played on the radio, and I vaguely listened to the storytelling in the background. Mostly I sat and stared at the faint outline of the passing trees still luminous from the sunset while the unintelligible words uttered from the speakers lulled me almost to sleep.

The storytelling was followed by a brief piano interlude; it was simple and peppy. I took a deep breath, and Drew took my hand as we drove on in silence along the deserted country road.

At the very end of the radio program, the musical guest for the week sang one final song. The acoustic duo Storyhill began to play the chords of their song "Paradise Lost." As the song began, Drew reached over and turned the volume up. We sat quietly as we took in the lyrics.

Everybody wants a piece of paradise
A house up on the hill with a view of heaven
Now everyone's here so close together
Paradise is lost and gone forever
When we were young we used to walk out in
those fields
And run forever in the backyard woods
Now the old trails disappear in
neighborhoods
With streets named after what's gone
for good

For the next three minutes, I sat completely transfixed. Two acoustic guitars strummed together accompanying the simple melody and harmony. The song filled me with peace and also an intense longing. The lyrics put into words a deep ache I had: a simplicity of life that I once had possessed that now seemed to be lost forever.

The longing I felt was amplified by the way the vocalists sang with passion and a strong conviction.

The lead singer held out the last note, and it was completely silent inside the car.

"Wow," I whispered after a few moments. I couldn't remember the last time I had felt so touched by a song. I was literally rendered speechless as if I had just witnessed an incredible mountain view that couldn't be captured in words.

"That was really captivating," Drew added.

It really was. I once again was amazed at how deeply a secular song could touch my soul.

~

DREW and I were packing up to move to a new home. Staring at our large collection of CDs, I commented, "I'm going to get rid of some of these. I never listen to them." I was specifically referring to the large compilation of CCM albums I had acquired through the years.

"No! Don't get rid of them. You never know when you might want to listen to them again." Drew had a fondness for all of his CDs and held tight to each one. He had also once purged his collection and like me had regretted his choice.

I gave him a look that said, *Never. Never again will I want to listen to this.* But I was tired from all the rest of the packing still to be done so I didn't argue. I tossed them into another cardboard box and forgot about them.

I went through a period of utter disdain for Christian music. My anger at being strung along by a marketing scheme for so long wouldn't allow me to say a single kind thing about the genre. If I heard even one measure of CCM, I would fly toward the radio, desperate to make it stop.

But after several years of processing, my heart is slowly beginning to soften. Many Christian artists are genuine and pour their heart into their music. Musicians like Nichole Nordeman and Andrew Peterson continue to inspire me. They have a way of artfully portraying the struggles and beauty of their faith without making it feel contrived.

I thought back to recording with Steven Curtis Chapman, how kind he was that day and how genuine he felt. It had been years since I had purchased one of his albums, yet I still felt a connection to his music. And even though I only spent a couple of hours with him, I honestly felt that he was one of those artists that genuinely loved Jesus and wanted to use his music to honor Him.

Just as 90s alternative music takes me back to high school, some Christian songs remind me of a time when my heart was on fire for Christ. Although my view ended up being a bit distorted, that love was very real.

Once settled into our new home, Drew set about unpacking

all of our CDs. It became quite the eclectic collection when we married and our albums merged together. My acoustic singer-songwriters commingle with his rap and R&B albums. Bach and Handel linger nearby Beck and Dr. Dre.

Drew unpacked each album and put them on display on a bookshelf in our living room. I browsed through this collection and was actually glad that Drew talked me into keeping all those Christian CDs. They, along with my other albums, are the story of my life summed up in jewel cases. I thumbed across the spines and cringed at the overly Jesus-y titles like *A Maze of Grace*. I looked farther and saw a few that softened my heart: Bebo Norman's *Myself When I Am Real*, Caedmon's Call's *Long Line of Leavers*, and The Normals' *Better Than This*. I traced the spine of each jewel case and remembered the songs that once touched me so deeply.

I slipped Andrew Peterson's *Love & Thunder* into the player. Looking at the track list, I flipped to track nine: "The Silence of God." Familiar chords filled the room. The lyrics broke through my cynical soul. Tears even stung my eyes and not the usual ones of frustration.

> *And if a man has got to listen to the voices of*
> *the mob*
> *Who are reeling in the throes of all the*
> *happiness they've got*
> *When they tell you all their troubles have*
> *been nailed up to that cross*
> *Then what about the times when even*
> *followers get lost*
> *Cause we all get lost sometimes*

It wasn't a song about how wonderful Jesus is or how glorious it is to worship Him. It was an honest acknowledgement of the times that faith is hard and sometimes painful.

Those words perfectly described where I was in my faith journey. As I listened, I was reminded of the many songs and Christian artists that touched my heart in a very real way. There were artists who were creating real art, untouched by the marketing machine of CCM.

By purging my music during my teenage years, I believed I was doing good things for myself. I wanted to look beyond the negative messages I was surrounded by in some of those 90s alternative hits. But I took it to the extreme. Just as bad movies and books can seep into the soul of a Christian, I have seen how the good things can also bleed in and brainwash. My CCM blanket had wrapped me in so tightly. I surrounded myself with those songs. The beauty that was to be found in other music had no chance of getting in.

I'd like to blame the CCM industry for all of this. But the truth is that nobody forced me into this. No one made me listen to Christian music or purge my CD collection. It was my choice. I thought listening to only Christian music would protect me and make me a better Christian. Instead, it made me un-relatable and pretentious.

I emerged slowly from my Christian cocoon. I didn't arise a beautiful butterfly. Instead I felt like an injured moth, slowly slinking out, crawling toward the sun, desperate to feel the warmth again.

24

I AM NOT A JUKEBOX

After tour, I worked as a barista. I learned to appreciate the art of latte foam and a good espresso tamp. I also became desperately addicted to really good coffee. It was a fun job, but the morning rush was a tad stressful.

At the register, streams of people would flow in and out. It was a constant rush of the un-caffeinated coming for their fix. Sadly, many people would place their order without ever making eye contact. They shoved debit cards in our faces.

"Medium cappuccino, skim milk."

"Small iced hazelnut latte, extra shot."

"Large black coffee."

My co-worker turned to me one morning and hissed in frustration, "I am NOT a vending machine!" I smiled back in understanding. I related to her annoyance. It's like people forgot there was a person attached to these coffee-crafting hands.

I thought of that moment a couple years later at my next job.

"Sing for us!!!"

I heard the gravelly voice come from a few rows behind me. I gritted my teeth and gripped the steering wheel tighter.

Chatter among the other passengers almost drowned it out, but then she said it again, louder.

"Hey, Jamie! Sing for us!"

"Not while I'm driving!" I said in a sing-songy voice through clenched teeth. I thought to myself, *I'm a little busy trying to not drive this damn van into a ditch!*

I had been working in the activities department of the senior living community for two years. I coordinated parties like luaus and country hoedowns, embellishing our large dining room with brightly-colored table clothes, banners, and festive decorations that hung from each chandelier. I hosted Happy Hour twice a month, where the residents nibbled on cheese and crackers and got buzzed on cheap wine. I called the Bingo numbers and served as a referee for bocce ball. I also drove them in a large 14-passenger van to lunches and dinners out. One time while driving them home from a steak dinner, the entire group sang drinking songs behind me. They had all had a couple drinks with dinner and were a little tipsy. I couldn't help but laugh.

Music was a part of my job too. We did sing-a-longs as I strummed guitar, often with one or two dozing off in the front row. (During one sing-a-long, I watched a resident pull out her teeth, examine them, and pop them back in.) I also conducted a bell choir, singing classic songs from the 30s and 40s while they dinged chords under me.

The residents loved to hear me sing, and they would tell me over and over how beautiful my voice was. One resident in particular would ask me, or rather demand I sing, every time she saw me.

When I was passing in the hall on the way to my lunch break.

"Sing for us!"

When I was carrying a heavy folding table after a party and a 10-hour workday.

"Sing for us!!"

When I was recovering from a cold and a nasty cough.

"Sing for us!!!"

When I was feeling really tired and spent and tender and only wanted to hide under the desk in my office.

"SING FOR US!!!!"

There were days that I wanted to turn to her and shout, "I am *not* a jukebox!"

I felt like she didn't see me but only saw the music I produced. It was as if she simply wanted to push a button and hear my voice emerge.

It felt like that at church too. Although I love and treasure my vocal gift, I became resentful of it. Even though my soul aches if I don't sing, the sheer act of people constantly asking me to do it made me not want to do it. I couldn't handle the constant requests, so I crossed my arms, stomped my feet, and declared, "*No.*"

Every time I went to church, some well-intentioned soul would declare how I needed to be back up on stage. I hadn't had the energy to return since coming home from tour. At first, it was not having the physical energy. Tour had taken so much of me that I didn't feel physically able to sing in front of people.

But once the physical energy returned, I found that I still didn't have the emotional energy. After processing through the grief of my kids, I found the horde of resentments that had been festering, and I didn't know what to do with them. Since so many of those resentments were geared toward the church, I knew I couldn't get back on stage. Nobody could comprehend that the mere idea of it made me want to burst into tears.

I felt that people only wanted my voice. It didn't seem that anyone was genuinely interested in me. I needed a break to allow myself a chance to simply sit and be without pressure of having to perform. I needed rest. I needed time to reflect and breathe. I was trying to live out, "Don't do, just be."

And yet, people kept telling me how I needed to return to the stage.

When I was at one of my lowest points, the time when I felt the most vulnerable, people only wanted me to give. And maybe I should have. Maybe I should have taken the low points and let God work through me. Maybe I should have marched back to that stage and snatched the microphone from the stand.

But I felt frozen in exhaustion, in fear, in doubts. How do you continue to serve with the gift that feels like it is crashing in around you? I couldn't sing the contemporary worship songs the church was asking me to sing. It was the very music that was causing the internal conflict within me.

I felt like I was being selfish by hoarding my gift. I was supposed to be serving my church and giving to the community. I had longed for so many years to sing for God. Now I had chances to do that, and I was running away. I wanted nothing to do with it. The drastic switch confused me. Why wasn't I grateful for my gift and chance to serve?

I couldn't escape the fact that I was burnt out. I was tired and resentful of the way the church demanded constant service. I had just spent three years on tour, devoting my life to teaching music and sharing the gospel. Since returning home, I had begun a job where I served senior citizens, and often it was emotionally draining. I needed refilling, and I felt that the church was just demanding my voice. Although I knew I desperately needed the rest, I still couldn't shake the guilt.

I thought about the parable of the talents. It was one of Jesus's many stories that I had read over and over the past 15 years.

A rich man goes away and gives money to his slaves. To one, he gives five pieces, to another he gives two, and to another he gives one. The first two slaves go off and invest their money and make more, apparently in some sort of Jerusalem stock market. The last slave, out of fear or laziness or maybe bitterness, takes his one piece of money and buries it. When their master returns, he praises the first two for their ingenuity and hard work ethic. When the last one confesses to burying his piece, he is chastised. Worse than that, the master condemns him to a place with weeping and gnashing of teeth. Wherever that is, it doesn't sound like a happy place.

The moral of the story is that we all have God-given talents and we need to use them to further God's kingdom. The more we use, or give back those talents, the more God will gift us. At least that's what I had always been taught.

I felt like that pathetic slave who hurried off to bury his one measly talent in the dirt. My refusal to sing was like burying the talents God gave me. I felt as if God was chastising me for not using them. Those Bible stories that I had treasured and studied for so long were telling me I was being selfish. The guilt crashed in on me.

But it was so hard to sing when I felt forced. It took away all the joy. I felt like an empty shell of a voice, notes plugged together in a seamless melody devoid of emotion. So I continued to hide in the back during worship, praying desperately to feel a bit of the glory that I had once felt.

Two years later, I did return for a brief time as a worship leader, but the burn out quickly returned. I led the songs that spoke to me, which were generally slower, quieter, and more introspective. Within a couple months, I was encouraged to lead more upbeat and energetic songs.

A congregant submitted an email to the leadership that said, "The music's been great, but it lacks the joyful feeling of celebration that used to be there." Because of that one email, I was told to lead songs of celebration. This was discouraging because I thought I had been. I didn't think a song needed be loud and upbeat in order to be celebratory.

I grew frustrated again at the need to over-extrovert at every church service, but I did as I was told and included more loud and animated songs. Once again, I felt myself trying to lead in a way that was not genuine for me. I felt like I was leading a performance instead of a worship service.

What was ironic was that I could now see the energetic, engaged worshipers I had longed for years during my first stint as a worship leader. I found myself longing for the quiet people, the ones with a quiet look of contentedness. Now I couldn't see beyond the people in the first few rows, some with hands raised high and tears running down their faces, and others dancing back and forth in the aisles. I felt like a fake standing in front of these energized people. I was putting on a show, a performance, just giving them a little pick-me-up from their weeks.

I grew more and more uncomfortable in front of that microphone. I longed to cower in the back row again. So once again I stepped away, desperate for a chance to feel the passion of music again.

It didn't return until I found myself surrounded by a hundred other voices.

The longer I stayed away from music the more my heart ached to sing again. I knew I needed to find some way to invite music into my life again. One of my Facebook friends posted about being a part of the Tallahassee Community Chorus. She was one of the worship leaders that had been passive-aggressively fired years before. I knew that through that choir she had found a beautiful outlet for her musical talents. The thought of joining the choir had been tugging at me for a while. I decided to finally take the plunge.

I walked in the door that first night nervous yet excited. I hate crowds of strangers, but I was so desperate to feel the energy of music again that it forced me through the awkwardness and into my seat.

My friend greeted me with a huge hug and a small gift bag of pumpkin spice coffee and tea. The card read, "I'm so glad you're here!" I smiled, glad that I was there too.

We sang familiar warm-ups, and I was transported back to my high school choir days, to the time where music grabbed hold of my heart. Five notes up the scale and then back down. We sang arpeggios and octave jumps. We buzzed our lips to work on breath control. I remembered standing in front of my beautiful African children singing zing-a-mamas to warm them up before a concert.

We pulled out our first piece of music, a piece that our conductor Dr. Thomas had composed. I sat up straight with my back off the chair, held my music high, and took a deep breath while the piano started the intro. The simple act of sitting in the straight-backed posture of a singer made me feel better.

As the choir began to sing, I almost fell out of my chair. I forgot how beautiful a sound a choir could create. The rich bass tones rose up and intermingled beautifully with the altos and tenors, and the sopranos I was surrounded by soared high into their notes. I remembered I was supposed to be singing too, and I gathered myself and found my part in the score.

There is something magical about singing with a choir. The sheer fact that simple human voices can create such sound, evoke such emotion, and cause your heart to stir so strongly is amazing to me. The sound of such different voices and timbres all combining together remind me of a beautifully-baked pie. The different flavors mingle together in the oven and emerge a mouthful of deliciousness: crisp, buttery crust and tart fruit, melted sugar and cinnamon. In the same way I savor each wonderful bite of pie, I love to lose myself in the midst of the harmonies and crescendos in the middle of a choir. A good choir is like apple pie for the ears.

Every time I sing with a choir, I feel like I am home. It was in the Tallahassee Community Chorus that I began to discover my voice again.

Through singing Mendelssohn's *Elijah* and Schubert's *Mass in E Flat Major* I found myself quietly worshiping. As I scribbled my notes in the margins of the sheet music, I rejoiced in the fact that my voice could once again be lifted up to God.

Nestled amongst those hundred other voices, I lifted my voice unto the Lord.

PART VIII

SUSPENSION

25

WORSHIP ANYWAY

It was Easter morning, 2012. Instead of the joy that this morning usually brought, I felt apathy. Drew and I had recently floated from church to church, trying to find the best place for our longing hearts to rest. I felt homeless.

We visited new churches, exploring different worship options. Church hopping is fun for a while, but on Easter, I just didn't have the energy to be a first-time visitor somewhere.

Since we felt like we had no church home, we were unsure of where to go. We settled on our old church, the place where we met and were married. I wasn't excited about attending because I was still tender from my past experiences with the ugliness of church politics. I was still angry from the way my friend had been treated when let go from her worship leader position. I was so livid at how easily she had been discarded that I had been unable to work through that resentment. Walking back through those doors was difficult.

Honestly, being in any church was difficult. My frustration at the music had bled into the other elements of any church service. I found myself judgmental of every piece: the preaching, the announcements, and especially the dreaded passing of the peace (every introvert's personal hell). Everything felt rote and routine with little sense of purpose.

When we arrived, a friend greeted us with a warm hug and asked if we would serve communion. I was hesitant as all of my old familiar yucky feelings began to arise. I don't take communion lightly.

I thought of I Corinthians 11, where Christians are instructed to examine themselves before taking the bread or drinking from the cup. Communion is a sacred time and should be treated as such. If I feel like even an inch of my heart is out of place, I don't take communion. I wasn't sure if I was ready to even take it, let alone serve it.

Drew was willing to serve. He looked at me for confirmation. I could have easily said no, and he wouldn't have questioned it. He was well aware of all that I was fighting in my heart. But I trusted his gut instinct, and I stepped out on faith. I agreed to serve.

Worship started out rough, and I reverted to my usual judgmental self. The sound mix was off, and all I heard were harmony vocals. Being married to a sound engineer had made me sensitive to things like the mix. As if being a music snob and noticing flat notes and bad diction wasn't enough of a worship spoiler.

The sermon that followed was good. Not mind-blowing, but good. I settled for good. I so often had problems focusing on the sermon and walked away completely unsure of how to apply it to my life. A good sermon that slightly spoke to my heart was better than the norm lately.

Communion began, and I felt those familiar frustrations. I did all that I felt I could do in the moment and offered them up to God. I had nothing more than irritations and agitation. I wished that I had a heart full of love and graciousness, but it just wasn't there and I couldn't force it to come. As much as I wanted to *want* to be at church, I would have rather been curled up on my couch at home.

Then, our pastor said something that stopped my wandering thoughts in their track.

"Even if you don't feel like it, come and worship."

So often I felt like worship was conditional. I'll do it when I feel the feelings, when the emotions are right. But I soon learned that time never comes.

The last thing I felt during worship was filled up. I more often felt empty, drained, and tired. For so long, worship was happiness, giddiness, and feeling close to God. Anything less was not real worship. I knew that was not true, but it's hard to push back against that lie when every other Christian around you is happy, giddy, and close to God.

I reminded myself that just because I felt tired and unworthy didn't mean I couldn't worship. It's not like God wouldn't accept my worship because it wasn't good enough. But many Sunday mornings I felt like that, like God wouldn't take what I brought.

Some days I felt like Cain.

In Genesis 4, there is the story of two brothers: Cain, a farmer, and Abel, a shepherd. Both brought an offering to God. Cain brought some fruits of the soil. Abel brought fat portions from some of the firstborn of his flock. God looked with favor on Abel's gift but rejected Cain's.

Between Cain and Abel, Abel brought the "better" sacrifice, which I had always believed to mean he brought the best he had, whereas Cain might have been holding out. When we worship, we should offer God the absolute best we have.

But what about when the best we have to offer isn't very good?

When I first read the story of Cain and Abel 20 years ago, I was puzzled. Cain was a gardener and worked with plants, so he brought the fruits of the ground to God. I liked veggies, so this seemed like a good gift to me. But God didn't look with favor on his offering; he looked with favor on Abel's instead. What was it that made Cain's offering not good enough?

There is more to the story, and the Bible doesn't really give us much detail on the state of Cain's heart (other than he killed his brother in a fit of rage after this incident, which I guess is a little glimpse into his character). He might have begrudgingly brought his offering while Abel brought his with a joyful heart. All we know for sure is that he was a gardener. That's what he did. He brought the fruits of his effort to God's feet. And he was rejected.

I think I understand why he was a little peeved.

That Easter morning, and many Sundays before it, I felt like Cain. I was trying to bring the best I had, but because I wasn't doing it like everyone else around me, it was rejected. I needed a little more blood, sweat, and tears in my worship.

I knew this was absolutely ridiculous. But when I was totally, completely honest with myself, I struggled with these things. I still do.

I'm not good enough.

I'm not trying hard enough.

If I worshipped with hands raised high and voice singing along to each and every worship song, then God would accept my offering and I'd feel better about my faith. If I was more joyful and proclaimed to the world all the good that God had given me, then all would be well.

In the very pit of this struggle, Sunday after Sunday I dragged myself to church with every ounce screaming internally, *DON'T MAKE ME!!!* I sat in the pews, feeling very little. I listened to the music and felt unmoved. I heard the sermon and was not able to relate any of it to my life. Communion began, the holiest of times that I used to love and anticipate every week. I still felt nothing. Tears of frustration stung my eyes. Surely I should be getting something out of this. I was afraid to approach the communion table because I didn't feel my heart was worthy enough.

So I eked out a prayer.

"God, I am not feeling anything right now. I'm numb. I'm tired. I'm frustrated. I want to feel and worship and be excited and I just can't. All I have is this half-hearted feeling. I'm trying, and I'm struggling. That's all I can lay at Your feet."

That Easter morning, I prayed that prayer. Then Drew and I approached the altar to accept the elements. Our pastor tore off a big chunk of the fluffy loaf and turned toward me. I cupped my hands together, and he placed the piece into my waiting palms. I felt the softness of the bread against my skin, and I closed my eyes as my pastor whispered.

"The body of Christ, broken for you."

He placed a piece of the bread into Drew's waiting hands. Then he picked up the wooden cup filled with purple juice, the sweet liquid that runs so deep with the symbolism of Jesus's blood. He brought the cup toward us and whispered, "The blood of Christ poured out for you."

Taking a deep breath, I dipped that hunk of bread into the sweet juice cup. I held my other hand out to catch the purple drops that fell. I opened my mouth and popped that bit of grace inside. I savored the taste of the grape soaked into the bread. After chewing a few times, I swallowed it down.

The remaining loaf was handed to me, and I turned to face the congregation. The sea of faces lay before me, many faces that I had stood before years ago as a worship leader. I felt relief that there was no microphone in front of me this time, just the body of Christ, broken for each of them.

One by one, each person came forward, hands outstretched, eager to accept the body and blood. I looked into familiar faces, faces that had smiled with joy at the news that I was going to travel with the African Children's Choir, arms that had hugged me in support as I prepared to fly thousands of miles from home. Their eyes sparkled as they looked into mine, and with no words spoken, I heard them clearly. They were glad to see me, happy that I was there. I tore off a heaping piece of the body for them.

"The body of Christ broken for you."

I looked at faces that I suspected had played a role in the passive-aggressive firing of my friend. Faces that sat in committee meetings where decisions were made that would crush spirits. Voices that chose not to speak up about the damage that could be done and also voices that said the words that sparked the decisions. I looked down at the bread and remembered that even though I was angry, they were still deserving of this grace.

"The body of Christ broken for you."

I looked into the eyes of people that had been there for my days of worship leading. People who had been supportive even as I struggled to find my voice and become comfortable with the way I led. People who brought song suggestions and others who sat quietly in the back rows, the way I now did. I smiled at them, placing their little piece of grace into the palm of their hands.

"The body of Christ broken for you."

I looked at the grinning faces of friends who knew both Drew and I intimately, the friends who threw their arms around us squealing in excitement at the news of our engagement. People who knew my struggles and loved me even more in spite of them or maybe even because of them. I grinned back at them as I handed the bread to them.

"The body of Christ broken for you."

I watched as downcast faces approached the altar. People who seemed hesitant and scared to lift their heads. I saw bags under eyes and caught glimpses of red eyes, possibly tinged from tears recently shed. They were obviously going through struggles. I wondered if any of them were in the place I was: wanting desperately to be anywhere but here. I tore off an extra big chunk of the bread for them.

"The body of Christ broken for you."

Through all the yuck and frustration, God was still there and waiting. I could feel my frustrations melt away. Holding the symbol of the body of Christ in my hands helped to put all that junk into perspective.

All I could offer that Easter morning was that meager prayer. And God accepted it. I realized that was enough. I trudged myself up that aisle amongst all those happy Christians who were squealing with joy over all God had done for them, and I dipped my bread into the juice. I accepted Jesus' gift and thanked God for the little bitty bit of peace I had managed to scrape up.

26

SECOND HARVEST

At the time of writing the first draft of this chapter, I hadn't been to church in a year. It wasn't an intentional decision. I took a break for a few weeks. I needed to step away, to rest, to sort through the mess of feelings in my head. I relished sleeping in an extra day. I lounged in bed and relaxed with my coffee, those two glorious acts that I couldn't partake in during the week.

It became habit. Sunday morning meant more sleep and blissful quiet. Weeks turned into months. My short break became the norm.

One rainy and dreary Sunday morning, several months into my church sabbatical, I lazily woke up and made my way to the French press. As I waited for the coffee to brew, I gazed out the back window and watched the trees sway in the breeze and listened to the soft pelt of the raindrops against the panes.

With my coffee cup in hand, I walked past Drew, who was watching a *South Park* rerun while reading the paper on his iPad. I didn't feel like watching TV and wanted a bit of quiet, so I went to my music room. Echoes of Cartman seeped through the closed door. I settled into the cozy armchair. That armchair was my safe space, where I penned many of these words and strummed my guitar when the words wouldn't come.

I cradled my mug and looked around the room. My journal lay on the side table, but I didn't feel like writing. Guitars hung on the wall, but I didn't want to play music either. I felt mopey, irritated, and restless. I couldn't put my finger on why. I sunk back into the suede fabric and took a sip of my coffee, sitting in quiet for a few minutes.

The rain continued to fall, and I closed my eyes and listened to the soft cascading against the windowpane next to me. I took a slow, deep breath, trying to sort through my head.

Then the reason for my mopey mood hit me. It was Sunday, and I wasn't at church. I had been gone for months, and it was like it was just now hitting me. I was coming out of denial for this grief, finally allowing myself to feel the sadness.

I was grieving church, but at the same time, the thought of returning made me want to cry. Being surrounded by people with happy faces, declaring how blessed they were. I just couldn't do it.

I missed feeling excited about church. It used to be the place where I felt most whole. Now I couldn't walk through the doors without feeling like I was breaking in two.

My introverted soul was exhausted. I had grown weary of dealing with people. Since returning home from tour, I had bounced from job to job. After working at the senior living facility, I spent two years working for a homeowners' association, an organization that is not a popular entity in many eyes. I answered endless phone calls from angry homeowners wondering why they received a letter asking them to mow their lawn or pressure-wash their home. Others were upset when I asked them to provide proof of residency for access to the neighborhood pool. I was yelled at, spoken down to, and told to go fuck myself (among a variety of other colorful phrases). I came home in tears many afternoons.

I was tired of meanness, passive aggressiveness, and rudeness. I crashed into my couch at the end of each day and wanted nothing to do with anyone. And while I knew that within the church there were precious people who carried none of the above characteristics, I no longer had the energy to seek them out.

The tragic irony was that I missed community. I desperately longed for it. I knew that my tendency was to hole away into myself, to isolate until it was unhealthy. I needed people around me who would pull me out of myself. Yet, the thought of being amidst a sea of people making small talk chased me away. I wanted to get back to that place where I felt comfortable sharing more than the weather. It's so worth it when you're there but such a struggle to get there.

I missed being with people who got me, who would ask how I was doing and want a genuine answer. I missed more than awkward hugs. I missed not having to put the fake smile on because I just didn't want to get into it. I found these people years ago through church choir rehearsals and praise band practices, in Bible studies and at women's retreats. Somewhere along my journey, they slipped away. Or maybe I did.

I thought back to nights spent at church choir rehearsals, laughing as we sang together. I remembered the cheers of encouragement as I learned a new solo that would accompany the choir anthem that week. I remembered silently praying at a women's retreat when I felt gentle hands on my shoulder. I knew they belonged to a woman I looked up to, a woman who had been in my life for years, who had prayed for me for as long as I'd known her. I remembered a Bible study where one of the participants tragically lost her young husband of only a few short years. When she found the strength to return to the study, we all surrounded her, praying over her and crying at the same time. We snottily blew our noses and went through an entire box of tissues as we lifted her up and supported her.

Along with community, I found that I missed worship. I missed being challenged, hearing words of wisdom and conviction. As much as I had grown to dislike modern worship music, I missed feeling connected to something powerful and singing along with passion. Church had given me a place to sing. It had helped me discover my voice.

My disillusionment at CCM culture and boredom with Christian music had affected the other pieces of my faith life. The disillusionment had grown to anger and then to full-fledged resentments against the church. I was resentful at the way I had been made to perform during worship services, how I felt my voice had only been used to create the proper worshipful atmosphere. Every time I entered church and the music began, I was reminded of those deeply-seated resentments even though I wasn't on stage. And since so much of the church services I had attended were built around that energetic, CCM style worship, it was hard to escape those resentments.

So I walked away. It was easier to avoid the resentments than deal with them.

I let out a deep sigh and took another sip of coffee. I closed my eyes and whispered a meager prayer. As my eyes opened, my gaze fell upon my Bible. It was lying on the ottoman in front of me. I couldn't remember the last time I had opened it.

I set my mug down and gingerly lifted the hefty book from its resting place. It wasn't the King James Bible my mother had bought or the paperback version I had discovered in college; I had worn that one out from so much use that pages had fallen out. This was a large, leather-bound Bible with gold pages and a small Hebrew & Greek dictionary in the back. I had bought it shortly after college. I had voraciously studied that book, looking up the original text of passages. Now the thought of studying Greek words made me tired.

I ran my finger over the leather cover and softly traced the spine. I thought back to the days where it sat on my nightstand and was the first and last thing I read each day. Now it was tossed upon the ottoman, forgotten about for months. I touched the golden edges then flipped through the whispery pages. I passed through genealogies and the poetry of the Psalms. I noticed small coffee stains, memories of morning devotions from years past. I saw the red-letter words of the New Testament and stopped flipping. I missed reading Jesus' teachings.

My eyes fell upon the parable of the sower, a story Jesus shared with his followers.

This characteristically-cryptic tale tells the story of a farmer sowing seeds. He sprinkles the seeds over the ground, and as he goes, the seeds land in different places. Some fell on the path, where the birds quickly ate it. Other seeds fell on rocky ground, where the plants quickly bloomed but then withered just as quickly. Other seeds fell on thorns, which choked out the plants. The rest of the seeds fell on fertile soil, and the plants bloomed and prospered.

I knew this parable well, having read it dozens of times. I led a children's musical years ago that was based on this parable. In simple yet thoughtful lyrics, the musical taught the lesson of the sower: Christians with strong roots will bear much fruit.

Every time I had read this parable over the last 15 years I had proudly thought how lucky I was to have had the Word fall on my fertile soil. I had abundant faith and thoroughly understood the Word. I felt sorry for the poor saps with weedy and rocky lives. How sad to miss out on this glorious message!

My eyes welled up with tears as I realized that maybe I was the one with the rocky ground. I received the gospel with joy, but I didn't last long.

I sifted through the gravel and found the small pieces of faith that were left. I wasn't sure if I had another chance. Could

I take these small fragmented seeds and plant again? Or had the troubles of this world, the confusions of my mind completely taken over any chance of real faith?

I closed my Bible and held it to my chest. I wanted a second harvest, but I wasn't sure where to start. I had a gnawing suspicion it was going to involve church. I knew that I didn't need to attend church to worship, but that desperate longing for community kept eating away at me.

The thought of walking through church doors made me wince. I was not ready to feel the frustration again, to be reminded of how resentful I still felt toward Christian culture. It was easier to feel numb, to deaden my senses with another scroll through my Facebook feed, trying to ignore the ache in my heart. I tried to shake the feeling that something was missing, that something was drastically wrong. I feared the thing that could fix it might, instead, make it worse.

I felt too tired to face this head on, but I was also weary of being stuck in this place. I was exhausted from this place of not feeling, of apathy and indifference. I needed to do something.

I was scared to keep digging. I was afraid if I did, I would lose all my faith. I felt like it was holding on by a thread. Little pieces had given way, and I desperately held on to the strands that were left. I was afraid to let go.

Christianity made up so much of me. CCM in particular had been my life, my passion. I didn't know how to define myself anymore. I didn't know which parts were real. So much of it fell away, nothing more than pomp and façade. I was clinging to the parts that held me together. What if I dug in more and found that the rest of it was fake?

I didn't know what to do with that. Jesus was my rock. What if He really wasn't who I thought He was? What if He wasn't what He promised He would be?

My coffee grew cold as I continued to clutch my Bible. I thought of those many mornings where I pored over the words of this book, praying to make myself more Christ-like and to be filled with more honesty and patience and love. Each prayer had emboldened me, made me feel stronger and surer.

I became angry as I thought of the struggles over the last several years. Faith used to be so easy. I was so tired of this constant fight, always trying to worship the right way and feel the right feelings. A lone tear escaped my right eye. My chest heaved slightly as sobs threatened to overtake me.

"God," I whispered to the ceiling. "When did faith become so hard? Why can't I seem to move past this?"

Silence.

"Please... help me. I don't know what to pray anymore or even what to believe. Are you even there?"

I laid my head against the soft cushion behind me. Letting out a loud sigh, I clutched the Bible tighter.

"Do you even care?"

More silence.

I was frustrated at the lack of answers and the fact that my prayers did little to fill my empty soul. I knew that God wasn't going to audibly answer my prayers, but I had hoped for a little peace at least.

Despite my frustration, I wanted a chance at that second harvest. I remembered that the God I had served for so long was a beautiful God of second chances. If this God really was real, He would never tell me that I couldn't try again. I would never hear that there was no hope. I could sit here and continue to mope, or I could dive in and deal with it.

It wouldn't be easy. Planting and harvesting take a lot of work. The dead plants on my kitchen windowsill reminded me of that. The seeds need nurturing and attention. I couldn't just put them under dirt and sit back and wait for faith to bloom.

Holding my Bible to my now pounding heart, I prayed again.

"Jesus, I'd like to try for a second harvest."

I didn't know what the new harvest might look like. I wasn't sure if it would be fruitful or if I would come up empty with nothing to show but fistfuls of dry dirt. For all I knew, I could emerge on the other side realizing that this really had all been fake, one big ruse told throughout the centuries. But I knew that I was tired of sitting in this place of cynicism, constantly fighting back tears and trying to tell myself it was all okay.

And from all I knew of Jesus, all the stories and parables, the kind words and harsh judgment spoken through red letters, I knew that I wasn't ready to give up on Him just yet.

27

SUSPENDED CHORD

Every Monday night, no matter how tired I am from my workday, I grab my manila folder stuffed with sheet music and head to rehearsal with the Tallahassee Community Chorus. I sing second soprano, the part directly under the first sopranos. The first sopranos sail away at notes on staves high above the treble clef. I've sung first soprano for years and relished in the fact that I could pop up to those high notes. But with age those notes have become harder to reach, and I have settled into a slightly lower register.

Second sopranos often sing with the firsts, so I still get a few chances to work on my higher range. But some songs contain a second soprano harmony part. Since I've been the top part of a choir for so long, I'm not used to singing harmony. It took practice for my voice to settle into a part that wasn't the melody.

One late November evening, we rehearsed a song for our Christmas concert. The song "Ring Out, Ye Bells" was a brand-new piece composed by two doctoral students at Florida State University. We sight-read through our parts, and there was a luscious second soprano harmony part. Nestled in between the first sopranos and altos, I happily settled into the harmony.

And then we sang a suspended chord.

In a suspended chord, the third note is omitted, replaced usually with either a perfect fourth or a major second. There is dissonance, which creates tension. A suspended chord feels like it is meant to resolve. There is one note that is not quite right, that sounds slightly off. That one note is meant to slowly, gracefully, and beautifully move down (or up) one note. It resolves, and you breathe a sigh of relief. The tension is gone.

I used to listen to the alto part in high school choir with envy. They always got the note in the suspended chord that needed to resolve. Singing that out of place note is an amazing thing. Your voice tugs at you, wanting so much to slide into that resolution. The tension in the chord, all the emotion, lies in that one note.

Now, as I sat surrounded by my community of fellow singers, I had that note. I was so excited to sing it. I belted it out loud, leaning into the tension that it held and listening to the dissonance created with the first sopranos. The dissonance was like an itch that I needed to scratch but couldn't quite reach.

The phrase held the suspended note slightly longer than I expected, and I kept trying to resolve the chord too early. My voice kept moving down a note a couple beats too soon. After singing the phrase a few more times, I finally counted correctly and held it for the correct number of beats. It felt glorious to hold that note and for that long. The phrase had more musical depth with that longer suspension, more apprehension and longing. Resolving the chord too early stole that moment.

I'm doing the same thing with my disillusionment, with this deconstruction and reconstruction of my faith. I keep trying to get it to resolve. I feel as if this struggle will never make sense until it's wrapped in a pretty bow. When I no longer have doubts about my faith, all will be well.

In so many great symphonies, concertos, cantatas, and even three-chord worship choruses, the final chord is a moment of beautiful resolution. All of the intricacies of the piece are wrapped up pretty when the final chord rings through the air. The emotions felt and the heartstrings that were tugged with each note played, it all comes down to that last note. We have been taken on a musical journey, and now we can rest. There is closure in that chord resolution. We long for closure.

I keep waiting specifically for the major chord resolution. In so many of the CCM songs I treasured, there were major chord resolutions. It felt right because major chords are happy. It wraps up a song in a cheerful and neat way, like a Hallmark Christmas movie. It feels final, complete. I realize now that the major chord resolution isn't the only way to finish a musical phrase. It isn't the only way to live life either.

Major chords are nice, but songs with only those chords don't have much "flavor." Music becomes boring, repetitive, and predictable. I'm a sucker for a good minor chord or even a diminished chord. Diminished chords sound ugly, but they certainly convey the intended emotion. My personal favorite in the chord family is that beautiful suspended chord.

Sometimes a piece of music ends on a suspended chord. You're left wondering. It's wide open with no resolution. The tension hangs in the air, and it's palpable.

As I continue to struggle with the questions, the uncertainties, and the disillusionment, I keep getting stuck on the suspended chord.

I may never figure this out. I will probably always have doubts. I'm not always going to feel like I'm put together. That suspension may never resolve.

I take hope in the fact that there is beauty in suspended chords. They bring drama, life, and intense emotion to music.

Nichole Nordeman is one of the few Christian artists that I still deeply respect. She has a song called "Gratitude" that was one of my favorites during my CCM days. The song is about being grateful in all circumstances, even if they don't end up exactly like we prayed or hoped for.

The second chorus states:

We'll give thanks to You
With gratitude
A lesson learned to hunger after You
That a starry sky offers a better view if no
roof is overhead
And if we never taste that bread...

The song ends on a sort of suspended chord, and it's beautiful. It leaves room for wondering and gives space for the listeners to hear their own story in the song. It never fully resolves, and I love it.

I loved the song so much that when I was in college, still eagerly attending church every week, I sang it for special music. I went to LifeWay and bought the accompaniment track. When I got home to rehearse, I was incredibly disappointed. At the end of the song the cheesy karaoke accompaniment had resolved the suspended chord. I couldn't believe it. Whoever had put this track together took it upon themselves to rewrite Nichole's brilliant ending and forced resolution where there was never meant to be any. I felt cheated.

I'm learning to embrace the suspensions without looking for the tension to subside, without forcing the resolution. I'm willing to hang out in the beauty of this chord and of this space and place in my life.

On the night of my community choir's Christmas concert, we performed "Ring Out, Ye Bells." I sang the second soprano harmony part, and especially that suspension, with everything I had. I reminded myself not to rush through the moment.

Other choirs from Florida State University's College of Music joined us in that concert. I sat in the audience, waiting for my choir's turn to perform our other songs. In the darkened auditorium, I listened as each choir performed their pieces. I was drawn especially to the a cappella pieces. I listened with rapt attention as their voices blended beautifully together, gliding between each pitch and artfully sewing each phrase together with the notes they sang. And each time they came to a suspension, I closed my eyes and breathed. I waited for the resolution, but I also hoped that it wouldn't come. The sound was so beautiful it made my heart ache in a really good way. It was like a rainstorm when you long to see the sun again but also want to stay in the peaceful moment of the rain falling. I wanted to stay in that moment of intense beauty, wanted to soak in the passion I felt toward the music.

When I opened my eyes, the suspension resolved, and I blinked back tears. The beautiful tension was gone, and I honestly kind of missed it. And some of the suspensions in that a cappella music resolved so softly, so gently that I wondered if it had even resolved at all. Like a gentle breeze that rustles through the soft grass, you know the breeze is there, but you can barely hear it blow.

The sounds of the suspension reminded me of why I have always felt drawn to music, why I turn to singing when I feel empty or joyful. Why I sing when I feel anything at all and also why I sing when I feel nothing. Music gives expression to those feelings I cannot voice.

I believe that God is still there in those moments of tension and struggle. The suspension is where He really works. It's where I really see what He can do. And, if I let Him, I think it's where His love is the strongest.

I have a long way to go. I still don't like going to church. Even though I've been convicted to return, my attendance is sporadic at best. I'll attend for a week or two and then take another month off. I still struggle with what church to call "home." I know I don't need to be in church to properly worship, but I also know the importance of fellowship and corporate worship. I know my faith isn't defined by church attendance and yet Hebrews 10:24-25 still haunts me.

Whenever I work up the energy and courage to walk through the doors of church, my issues are there to meet me. They usually slap me right in the face, a vivid reminder that they are still not fully resolved. That suspended chord strikes yet again.

I long to feel the passion of my faith again and that excitement over cracking open my Bible and wondering what God has in store for me today. The peace of feeling a warm breeze on my cheek and knowing that it is God. The wonder of hearing a song and being able to quietly say, "Amen."

But I want to leave behind the simple mindedness that filled my life. I need to abandon the feeling that I have to be constantly surrounded by all things Christian to be a good Christ follower or even just a good person.

Where do I go from here? I have jumped onto the liberal Christian bandwagon, affirming LGBTQ people and culture (especially after several friends came out) and embracing feminism (I've met some incredibly bad-ass women in recent years). And yet, another part of me longs to nestle back into the inerrancy of Scripture, believing and taking every word literally that is printed in that holy book.

I want to sneer in the direction of every CCM artist, yet I know there is beauty to be found in every art, no matter how simplistic I may find it. I can't sneer. I need to offer the same endless grace that's been offered to me, by God and by those who have sat in the audience and heard me sing.

I will move forward. With the knowledge that Jesus has never left me, I will continue on. I will buoy myself up with the continued mysteriousness of this man. I will let myself be continually amazed at the fact that He simply cannot be boxed in.

He is more than four chords, but I believe that He loves to be worshiped in that simplicity as well as in the grand majesty of a full orchestra.

I may not always rise above my cynicism, but He will always meet me there. And then He humbles me back because He loves me too much to leave me wallowing in it.

And when the suspension comes, I won't try to force the resolution before it's ready. I will sing loud and lean into the dissonance.

Because I know there is beauty to embrace in the tension.

POSTLUDE

I'd desperately hoped that by writing I would come to a happy resolution. Once this book was complete, everything would click into place like that final puzzle piece. All would be well, and I could go back to feeling close to God. Worship music would once again be the soundtrack to our glorious relationship.

But just as I feared, I don't have those answers. I come only with questions, frustrations, and a little anger. My faith feels shaky, barely bolstered up by sporadic Bible reading and the occasional half-hearted prayer thrown at the ceiling. I know that I believe in God, but I don't always feel Him. I still feel so tender and raw.

I think back to the super Christian I used to be. I sip (or sometimes chug) a glass of wine and think of how far I've come. Or fallen. I don't know which is better, the saved little clueless college girl or the cynical adult. I'm proud of how I've grown, but there are days I wish I had a little more hope. And faith.

I'm not entirely sure how to move forward, so I'll just do it with baby steps, a day at a time. I'll take the questions, even the doubts, and move into a faith that I hope will one day prove richer, fuller than I thought possible.

I'll continue to lift my voice to God. It may not be on the church stage or even a song specifically directed to Him, but I know that wherever I sing, He listens.

ANOTHER WORSHIP SERVICE. The band wasn't together, and the vocalists fought each other through every song. The harmony was all over, and I couldn't find the melody. That's partly because I didn't know the song but also because the leader was doing a pretty poor job of singing it.

My defense mechanism is cynicism. I get so tired of the tears of frustration that come during worship, so I put up my wall. Brick by brick, the cynic in me cleverly and carefully constructs the wall so I don't have to feel. The numbness is easier than the feelings.

I listened to the poorly done music and snickered. I rolled my eyes at the vocalist singing a really random harmony. I sighed in frustration at the obvious typo on the PowerPoint. I felt a pang of pity for the poor guy running the PowerPoint because the leader jumped from chorus to bridge to verse with no sense of order.

My friend sat next to me. She too was less than impressed with the music. We whispered some snarky comments in each other's ears. I knew it was mean. I've been on stage, and I know how hard it is up there. But I was so glad to not be alone, so glad someone else sees the things I see.

I looked around. I saw a man sitting in the midst of a standing crowd, hands crossed in front, staring blankly in front of him. Others stood with lips barely moving as if going through the motions. Groups of people sat at the tables in the back. Some whispered to each other and completely ignored the show in front of them. Others sat quietly, fiddling with the coffee straws in their hands.

I looked toward the front, to the rows directly in front of the stage. There are the excited people, the ones with hands raised, heads thrown back, singing passionately. These are the people I saw from the stage when I returned as a worship leader. When I was up there, feeling a little bit empty, trying to put on a show, these were the only ones I saw. I wondered why I was the only one who wasn't feeling the words I was singing. Why I couldn't get into the passion of the repetitive melody we sang.

When I was on stage, it was hard to see past the bright lights and hear beyond the blaring guitars. I didn't see the disengaged people with blank stares. I didn't realize there were many that felt a little empty.

I wonder why we don't acknowledge the pain and emptiness more.

The band began their final song. It was a little quieter, a little mellower. The band eased up, and the vocalists backed off a bit. The song almost sounded pretty.

"It's easier to worship with a sweet child's voice next to you," my friend whispered into my ear.

I looked to her right side and saw a young girl, maybe 14, with eyes shut tight. She quietly sang the melody, her head tilted upward. Her sweet, unassuming, soprano voice drifted up to the heavens. For a moment, the band faded away, and her voice was all I heard, a tender declaration to her Savior.

This must be what God hears.

ACKNOWLEDGMENTS

To Jim Woods and Mary-Beth Goetzke, thank you for reading an early draft of this book. Those words were like writing vomit, all over the place and not always pretty. I appreciate you reading my story and helping to point me in a better direction.

To my editor Andi Cumbo-Floyd, thank you for making me dig deeper into this than I ever really wanted to. This story has more depth and focus thanks to you.

To Olivia Hahnel, thank you for your vision and artistic talent on the cover design.

To Travis and Derek, your college friendship meant the world to me. Thank you for challenging me in my faith and for the many CCM sing-a-longs. Creation '98 is still one of the best road trips I've ever taken.

To the pastors in my life: Betsy, Bob, and Jim. I am thankful for your leadership and for constantly pointing to the grace of Jesus. In the midst of all the church drama, you always seemed to rise above it. Thank you for showing me what strong, loving, and devoted Christian leaders look like. (And Betsy, thanks for the nudge to listen to something other than CCM.)

To Doc and Miss Bobbie, thank you for instilling such a

deep love of music. You helped plant the seed that will continue to grow for the rest of my life.

To my first FSU voice professor David Wingate, I was saddened to find your obituary as I wrote my first draft. Although you and I didn't always see eye to eye, I recognize your great musical legacy, and I'm thankful for the small way you contributed to mine. I hope that eternity is full of Mozart requiems.

To my second FSU voice professor Barbara Ford, you are one of the most beautiful souls I have ever met. I know I wasn't always easy to work with, but I would not be the singer I am without you. Thank you for being patient and showing me the beauty that lies in classical music.

To Skylor Brumbeloe, thank you for helping me identify the song "Paradise Lost" by Storyhill. You took my ramblings from a 2010 journal entry and pointed me toward the song I had vaguely described. You rock.

To Dr. André Thomas and the Tallahassee Community Choir, thank you for reminding me how much I love singing. Monday night rehearsals have become my sanctuary and my worship.

To my African Children's Choir "kids," I cannot express how thankful I am to have been a part of your lives. The years I spent with you were some of the best years of my life. You made me a better musician (and a decent soccer player). I cannot put into words how wildly proud I am of each of you and the amazing people you are becoming. Alex K, Brenda, Christine, Dorothy, Douglas M, Felista, Frank, Frankie, Gladys, Gorrett, Jane, Joan, Joseph, Junior, Lawrence, Martie, Martin, Maureen, Moriah, Peter, Ruth, Ruthy, Stella, Veneranda, Alex B, Carol, Cissy, Denis, Douglas R, Elizabeth, Emmanuel, Fiona, Galale, Gift, Hamisi, Joash, Jolly, Kidah, Lilian, Manuel, Martha, Mary, Masika, Moses, Mwikali, Prossy, Rebecca, Timothy, and Winnie: I love you.

To Emily, 2,900 miles won't stop you from being the best friend I could ask for. As I walked through so many steps of this journey, I knew that you were walking a similar path. Knowing that I wasn't alone brought me much comfort. Buses, luggage, lavender scented sachets, and taxidermy will always make me think of you.

To Mom and Dad, thanks for dragging me back to church. I am a better person because of it. And thank you for coming to countless choir concerts and solo performances. Your encouragement has pushed me closer toward my goals.

To Jen, thanks for all the fun drawings on church prayer cards. Thanks also for the theatrical Annie reenactments in the living room. I think those impassioned performances may have helped push me toward music.

And to Drew, thank you for your constant humor, patience, and encouragement over the last 8 years and several book drafts. I love you, baby. My book has finally found its way.

ABOUT THE AUTHOR

Jamie A. Kocur is an administrative assistant by day and a writer, singer, and songwriter by night. Her writing has been featured on blogs such as Quiet Revolution, The Mudroom Blog, and Clothe Your Neighbor As Yourself. For years, she processed her thoughts by writing her blog at rebootingworship.com, and much of her musings there were inspiration for *My CCM Soundtracked Life*, her first book. Jamie lives in Tallahassee, Florida with her husband Drew.

facebook.com/jamiekocurauthor

twitter.com/jamiekocur

instagram.com/jamie_kocur

Made in the USA
Coppell, TX
18 May 2021

55883744R00142